Women's Diaries and Letters of the South
Carol Bleser, series editor

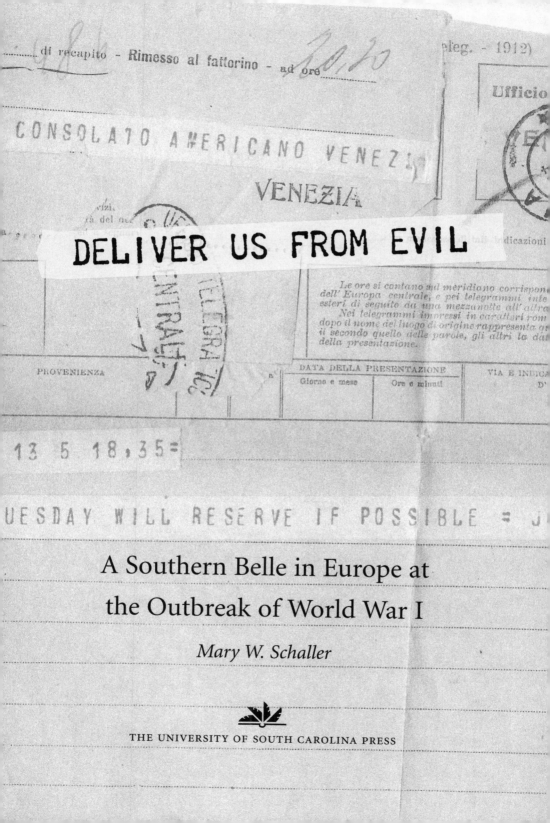

DELIVER US FROM EVIL

A Southern Belle in Europe at the Outbreak of World War I

Mary W. Schaller

THE UNIVERSITY OF SOUTH CAROLINA PRESS

© 2011 University of South Carolina

Published by the University of South Carolina Press
Columbia, South Carolina 29208

www.sc.edu/uscpress

Manufactured in the United States of America

20 19 18 17 16 15 14 13 12 11 10   9 8 7 6 5 4 3 2 1

Library of Congress Cataloging-in-Publication Data

Schaller, Mary W.
   Deliver us from evil : a Southern belle in Europe at the outbreak of
World War I / Mary W. Schaller.
       p. cm. — (Women's diaries and letters of the South)
   Includes bibliographical references and index.
   ISBN 978-1-57003-950-8 (cloth : alk. paper)
   1. Crawford, Nancy Johnson, 1888–1982. 2. Crawford, Nancy Johnson,
1888–1982—Correspondence. 3. World War, 1914–1918—Causes. 4. Americans—
Europe—Biography. 5. Principe di Udine (Steamship) 6. Kentucky—Biography.
I. Crawford, Nancy Johnson, 1888–1982. II. Title.
   CT275.C8746S45 2011
   976.9'0430922—DC22   2010044620

This book was printed on Glatfelter Natures, a recycled paper with 30 percent
postconsumer waste content.

Dedicated to my best friend, soul mate,
and wonderful husband, Martin Schaller,
Nancy Johnson Crawford's favorite grandson-in-law

No part of the Great War compares in interest with its opening.
WINSTON CHURCHILL

CONTENTS

ILLUSTRATIONS

SERIES EDITOR'S PREFACE

Deliver Us from Evil is the twenty-seventh volume in this series, now titled Women's Diaries and Letters of the South. This series includes a number of never-before-published diaries, collections of unpublished correspondence, and a few reprints of published diaries—a wide selection of nineteenth- and twentieth-century southern women's informal writings. The series may be the largest series of published works by and on southern women.

The goal of the series is to enable women to speak for themselves, providing readers with a rarely opened window into southern society before, during, and after the American Civil War and into the twentieth century. The significance of these letters and journals lies not only in the personal revelations and the writing talent of these women authors but also in the range and versatility of the documents' contents. Taken together, these publications will tell us much about the heyday and the fall of the Cotton Kingdom, the mature years of the "peculiar institution," the war years, the adjustment of the South to a new social order following the defeat of the Confederacy, and the New South of the twentieth century. Through these writings the reader will also be presented with firsthand accounts of everyday life and social events, courtships and marriages, family life and travels, religion and education, and the life-and-death matters that made up the ordinary and extraordinary world of the American South.

CAROL BLESER

Other Books in the Series

A Woman Doctor's Civil War: Esther Hill Hawks' Diary
Edited by Gerald Schwartz

A Rebel Came Home: The Diary and Letters of Floride Clemson, 1863–1866
Edited by Ernest McPherson Lander, Jr., and Charles M. McGee, Jr.

The Shattered Dream: The Day Book of Margaret Sloan, 1900–1902
Edited by Harold Woodell

The Letters of a Victorian Madwoman
Edited by John S. Hughes

A Confederate Nurse: The Diary of Ada W. Bacot, 1860–1863
Edited by Jean V. Berlin

*A Plantation Mistress on the Eve of the Civil War: The Diary of Keziah Goodwyn
   Hopkins Brevard, 1860–1861*
Edited by John Hammond Moore

Lucy Breckinridge of Grove Hill: The Journal of a Virginia Girl, 1862–1864
Edited by Mary D. Robertson

*George Washington's Beautiful Nelly: The Letters of Eleanor Parke Custis Lewis
   to Elizabeth Bordley Gibson, 1794–1851*
Edited by Patricia Brady

*A Confederate Lady Comes of Age: The Journal of Pauline DeCaradeuc Heyward,
   1863–1888*
Edited by Mary D. Robertson

*A Northern Woman in the Plantation South: Letters of Tryphena Blanche Holder
   Fox, 1856–1876*
Edited by Wilma King

*Best Companions: Letters of Eliza Middleton Fisher and Her Mother, Mary Hering
   Middleton, from Charleston, Philadelphia, and Newport, 1839–1846*
Edited by Eliza Cope Harrison

Stateside Soldier: Life in the Women's Army Corps, 1944–1945
Aileen Kilgore Henderson

From the Pen of a She-Rebel: The Civil War Diary of Emilie Riley McKinley
Edited by Gordon A. Cotton

Between North and South: The Letters of Emily Wharton Sinkler, 1842–1865
Edited by Anne Sinkler Whaley LeClercq

*A Southern Woman of Letters: The Correspondence of Augusta Jane
   Evans Wilson*
Edited by Rebecca Grant Sexton

Southern Women at Vassar: The Poppenheim Family Letters, 1882–1916
Edited by Joan Marie Johnson

Live Your Own Life: The Family Papers of Mary Bayard Clarke, 1854–1886
Edited by Terrell Armistead Crow and Mary Moulton Barden

The Roman Years of a South Carolina Artist: Caroline Carson's Letters Home, 1872–1892
Edited with an Introduction by William H. Pease and Jane H. Pease

Walking by Faith: The Diary of Angelina Grimké, 1828–1835
Edited by Charles Wilbanks

Country Women Cope with Hard Times: A Collection of Oral Histories
Edited by Melissa Walker

Echoes from a Distant Frontier: The Brown Sisters' Correspondence from Antebellum Florida
Edited by James M. Denham and Keith L. Huneycutt

A Faithful Heart: The Journals of Emmala Reed, 1865 and 1866
Edited by Robert T. Oliver

Elizabeth Sinkler Coxe's Tales from the Grand Tour, 1890–1910
Edited by Anne Sinkler Whaley LeClercq

Looking for the New Deal: Florida Women's Letters during the Great Depression
Edited by Elna C. Green

Dearest Hugh: The Courtship Letters of Gabrielle Drake and Hugh McColl, 1900–1901
Edited by Suzanne Cameron Linder Hurley

Selected Letters of Anna Heyward Taylor: South Carolina Artist and World Traveler
Edited by Edmund R. Taylor and Alexander Moore

ACKNOWLEDGMENTS

Nancy Johnson Crawford was my maternal grandmother and was like a second mother to me. I lived with my grandparents during the first six years of my life before my war-widowed mother remarried. After that, I spent summers with my grandparents throughout my childhood. I first learned of Nancy's experiences in Europe in 1961, when I lived with them during my senior year in high school. Later, in the 1970s and 1980s when I was an adult, Nancy fleshed out the stories of her life during numerous conversations.

Nancy always referred to her 1914 trip to Italy and her subsequent escape from World War I aboard the SS *Principe di Udine* as "the greatest adventure of my life." Consequently, she saved every scrap of paper that related to her experience. She intended to organize the souvenirs of her life into albums, but she had started only one before her death in 1982 at the age of ninety-four. I inherited Nancy's treasure trove of family papers. Most of the reference material for this book comes from this collection of letters, newspaper clippings, invitations, telegrams, guide pamphlets, photographs, and a remarkable little book, *The Sailing of a Refugee Ship* by Arno Behnke. This collection is identified in the footnotes as the Nancy Johnson Crawford Collection, (NJC Collection).

Arno Behnke began work on his memoir, "A little record of the voyage of the PRINCIPE DI UDINE," while the ship was still in the middle of the Atlantic. It was privately published by subscription in September 1914 for the passengers, among whom was twenty-six-year-old Nancy Johnson.

The author is especially grateful to Sarah Hartwell, Reading Room Supervisor, Rauner Special Collections Library, Dartmouth College Library, Hanover, New Hampshire, for her time and assistance in providing a photograph and biographical information on Arno Behnke. Her contributions to this story have been invaluable.

The author is also deeply grateful to Anne Talbott Willett, Nancy's youngest surviving niece, who inherited a great many of the letters that Nancy wrote to her family and who graciously gave them to me. Also, many thanks to Roscoe Campbell Crawford Jr., Nancy's surviving son, for his insights into his mother's life story and for his overwhelming support and enthusiasm for this project.

A "thank you" is owed to Carol and John Bessette. Their combined expertise in the history of Washington, D.C., at the turn of the twentieth century has been invaluable, and the research they did for me on the Great War is greatly appreciated.

I am also grateful for the time and information on the Gilded Age provided by the National Park Service Ranger guides at the Frederick Vanderbilt Mansion in Hyde Park, New York, especially Marge Farnett. Thanks and appreciation also to Bill Urbine and Tara McGill, archivists at the Roosevelt/ Vanderbilt National Historical sites, for their help, suggestions, and photographs of Frederick and Louise Vanderbilt during their European trip in the summer of 1914. I am deeply indebted to Julie Eldridge Edwards, curator of collections at Shelburne Farms, Vermont, for her research information and photograph of Frederick Vanderbilt.

Many thanks go to the amazing photography lab technicians at Protech Photo, Inc., of Alexandria, Virginia, for their excellent work and gentle care in printing Nancy's ninety-year-old negatives.

A grateful tip of the hat goes to Harry and Virginia Day, who did a superb job of scouring the manuscript for errors, as well lending their enduring support throughout this project.

Last, but hardly least, I am profoundly indebted to my husband, Martin Schaller, for his help in all aspects of the creation of this book. His suggestions, research, proofreading, image scanning, editing, and continual support are deeply appreciated more than mere words can express.

Prologue

Step back in time to August 4, 1914. Imagine yourself as a young American woman caught in Europe on the first day of World War I. You and your girlfriend are alone in Switzerland, thousands of miles away from your homes and families. The pampered, protected world that you have known all your life is crumbling around you. The banks are closed indefinitely; your letters of credit are now useless. There is no such thing as a credit card or an automatic teller machine. No one in Europe knows that your father is a wealthy, powerful man in the U.S. Congress. No one knows that you are a personal friend of President Woodrow Wilson. No one cares—now.

The borders are closed. Every European country is commandeering automobiles and horses for its armies. The trains run sporadically, if they run at all. Commercial air travel is unavailable. The only way to cross the Atlantic Ocean is by steamship, but the belligerent governments have requisitioned all the coal. Only a few ships are available in the neutral countries, and their shipping companies demand exorbitant prices to charter them.

Imagine that you have a mountain of baggage—and only sixty American cents in your pocket to get you safely home to the States.

In August 1914, a young Kentucky belle named Nancy Johnson and 120,000 other Americans scattered across Europe were enjoying their summer holidays when all hell broke loose.

This is the story of Nancy Johnson and of the *Principe di Udine,* the little ship that delivered her from the evils of war.

CHAPTER 1	*"Bred in Old Kentucky"*

Nothing in her upbringing or education prepared Nancy Johnson for the summer of 1914. Quite the opposite. During her first twenty-four years, the world was Nancy's satin oyster, and she, the pearl, nestled comfortably within it. Born on "one cold and frosty morning," November 2, 1888, Nancy saw her first light of day through the downstairs bedroom window of her parents' antebellum mansion a mile north of Bardstown, Kentucky.

The Johnson home was built in 1856 by Nancy's paternal grandfather, William Johnson V.[1] The house, a one-and-a-half-story Greek Revival design, was set back from the Louisville Road, now modern-day State Route 31, amid nearly one hundred acres of farmland. There were the usual number of dependencies for an antebellum farm of this size, including a detached kitchen, smokehouse, stable, barn, several slave quarters, and a pump well that still gushes fresh water. Most of these buildings stand today and were added to the National Register of Historic Places in 1980. The Johnson farm was known to raise the meanest but tastiest hogs in Kentucky as well as fine horses, guinea fowl, and peacocks. Nancy's father, Ben Johnson, decreed that "no chickens or children" were allowed to play on the velvety green front lawn. Several generations of children and chickens have generally ignored this rule.

A month after her birth, Nancy was baptized into the Roman Catholic Church at Saint Joseph's Proto-Cathedral in Bardstown. Her given name was Nannie Crow Johnson, in honor of her father's mother. Nannie Crow[2] of Boyle County, Kentucky, was the wife of William Johnson V. Family oral history relates that the first Nannie was "quiet" and much in the shadow of her flamboyant politician husband. However, Nannie Crow made her mark in history during the Civil War.

The members of the Johnson family were staunch Confederates, and Nannie was a member of the committee to select the design for the Confederacy's first national flag. When the final design was chosen, Nannie sewed a large flag that was raised on the front lawn of the Johnsons' home in early 1861. This Confederate flag raising reputedly attracted between three thousand and five thousand people. Also, in 1863, William and Nannie Johnson hid Confederate general John Hunt Morgan in their home for two days and a night following his successful escape from the Federal penitentiary in Ohio.[3]

Nancy's grandfather, William Johnson V, had died only a few months before she was born. William had studied the law under the legendary Ben Hardin, and he opened his practice in Bardstown before the Civil War. William had also served in the Kentucky legislature, where he became Speaker of the House. During the Civil War, William closed his practice and kept close to home, though he did see action briefly in the Confederate army, despite his advanced age of forty-five years. In December 1862, he accompanied a younger cousin, who had gone absent without leave to visit his family for Christmas, back to the Sixth Kentucky Infantry regiment in Tennessee. According to an account published in 1950, "William Johnson ran into the battle of Stone's River (December 31, 1862), in Middle Tennessee. Though he was unarmed, he picked up a rifle and some ammunition from a dead Union soldier. Then he aided the rear guard of the Confederate retreat. He shot at Union soldiers swimming across Stone's River until a shell fragment broke his leg at the knee. Thus he was mustered out, but never mustered in."[4]

After the war, William Johnson returned to his law practice. Among his clients were the infamous James brothers. Frank and Jesse James had been members of William Clarke Quantrill's irregular raiders during the Civil War, along with the Kentuckian brothers Donnie and Bud Pence. After the war, Frank and Jesse began their notorious bank-robbing careers, accompanied by Bud Pence. Donnie, on the other hand, returned to his family's farm near Bardstown and became a law-abiding citizen. By the 1870s, Donnie Pence was the sheriff of Nelson County, and William Johnson was his attorney. Whenever the James brothers needed to seek a safe haven, they fled to Bardstown, where they behaved themselves as much as possible. When they needed legal advice, they visited Johnson at his home outside of town. Family oral history relates that Nannie Crow Johnson would not allow such infamous men in her house, so William conducted his business with the James brothers under the black walnut tree by the pump house, where they quenched their thirsts with fresh spring water—and usually something stronger.[5]

William Johnson's brief Confederate service did not affect his return to politics. In 1868, he was elected Kentucky's lieutenant governor. The following year, Johnson served as acting governor for a short period, and today his name

Ben Johnson, Nancy's father, a Democrat from Nelson County, Kentucky, who served in the U.S. House of Representatives 1907–27

is listed among the governors of Kentucky. William and Nannie Johnson had four sons and a daughter who were born and reared in the family's home. Their eldest surviving boy was named Ben after William's mentor, Ben Hardin.

Ben Johnson, never "Benjamin,"[6] was a giant of a man both in physical stature and in Kentucky politics. Standing six-foot three-inches tall with piercing blue eyes, he was proud to call Nelson County his home. Following in his father's footsteps, Ben studied the law and graduated from the University of Louisville Law School in 1882 at the age of twenty-four. By that time, the ambitious young man had already amassed a personal fortune of $1 million from selling potatoes and orchard-grass seed, and particularly from shrewd real estate investments. Though Ben was a rich man in Kentucky, his wealth was considered insignificant by New York society's rarefied standards. Ward McAllister, a social majordomo who dined with the Astors and supped with the Vanderbilts, once observed that "a fortune of only a million is respectable poverty."[7] Despite McAllister's snobbish opinion, Ben thought that his financial future was secure. Blessed with a happy marriage and four children, Ben turned his brilliant intellectual powers and his driving ambition to politics.

In 1885, young Ben Johnson was elected to the Kentucky state legislature on the Democratic ticket. A contemporary newspaper article hailed him as a man "destined to steady and merited promotion at the hands of his party and friends."[8] This assessment was prophetic. Johnson won reelection in 1887 and was chosen as Speaker of the Kentucky House, again following in his father's footsteps. On July 10, 1893, he was appointed collector of internal revenue for the Fifth Kentucky District by President Grover Cleveland—a position that netted Johnson a widening circle of political influence not only in his native Nelson County but also throughout the entire state.

Ben Johnson had to be the first in every area he touched, and that included owning the latest gadgets and inventions of the time. In May 1892, he bought the first automobile in Nelson County as a thirty-fourth birthday present to himself. Since driver's licenses were not required at the time, Ben taught all his children how to drive the car as soon as they were big enough to reach the pedals and work the complicated gear shifts. In the early 1880s, he had also owned the county's first bicycle, a high-wheeled "boneshaker," with which he won several bicycle races. In 1889, the first telephone in Bardstown was installed in the Johnson family home, much to the delight of Nancy and her siblings.

Johnson's political star continued to rise. When his term as the Fifth District tax collector ended in 1897, Ben returned to the state capital in Frankfort, this time as a state senator. In 1906, at the urging of the Kentucky Democratic Party, he ran for a seat in the U.S. Congress.

Kentucky politics in the early 1900s was a rough-and-tumble affair. Though a teetotaler himself, Johnson set out kegs of Nelson County's finest bourbon at the entrances of the polling places on election day.[9] Large barrels of branch water, sweetened with brown sugar and fresh mint leaves, stood next to the kegs. A number of tin cups dangled nearby from handy nails. The none-too-subtle "Vote for Johnson" was painted on the kegs, cups, and barrels. The voter, before casting his ballot, was encouraged to quench his thirst with the compliments of Mr. Ben Johnson. If, upon exiting, the gentleman had voted the "right way," he was liberally rewarded with more of the ad hoc mint juleps.[10] Ben Johnson won his seat in the U.S. House of Representatives by a landslide.

This "frontier" attitude was found not only in Nelson County politics but also in its citizens' ways of life. "It was still the pernicious fashion in Kentucky to tote hardware, and young bucks in particular took pains not to be out of fashion," notes historian Alan Harlow.[11] Ben Johnson did not consider himself properly "dressed" for the day until he had pocketed his pistol. He even carried his gun with him while serving in the U.S. House of Representatives. He once drew his pistol in the House chambers when an infamous World War I "draft

Annie Mary
Kouwenberg
Johnson, Nancy's
mother, circa 1912

dodger," Grover Cleveland Bergdoll,[12] was testifying before a House committee in 1920. During the proceedings, Bergdoll made the mistake of calling Ben
Johnson a liar to his face. Johnson, who made honesty his religion, held his
personal honor above all else. He also possessed a fiery temper. That day, Ben
drew his pistol from his pocket. A fellow committee member restrained him
from shooting Bergdoll on the spot.[13]

Ben's wife, Annie Kouwenbergh Johnson,[14] concealed her own double-
shot, ivory-handled derringer in her muff whenever she drove her carriage
down the country mile into Bardstown.[15] In addition to carrying personal
weapons, the Johnsons also kept a loaded shotgun by the front door as late as
1933. Since the family home at that time was still situated in the open countryside, the gun was Ben Johnson's nocturnal "pest control" against intruders or,
in earlier times, his daughters' suitors who used to come by the house at night

The four children of Ben and Annie Johnson (clockwise): Hendy (b. 1890), Nancy (b. 1888), Ben (b. 1891), and Rebecca (b. 1887), December 31, 1896. Nancy is eight years old.

to serenade the three Johnson girls. Nancy claimed that her mother, as well as Nancy and her siblings, were all good shots.

Nancy, her two sisters, Rebecca[16] and Hendy,[17] and frail younger brother, Ben Junior,[18] grew up in the shelter of their well-appointed home with its velvet sofas, gilt-framed oil paintings, and antique French china. Pampered by an indulgent father and taught etiquette by their dignified mother, the children, except for little Ben, flourished in the clean country air, surrounded by beloved dogs, fine horses, and a flock of noisy peacocks. Nancy loved to ride horseback. By the time she was ten years old, she was a proficient horsewoman and enjoyed cantering across the fields of the family's plantation. Occasionally, however, she encountered difficulties.

In a letter to her maternal grandmother, Rebecca Cox Kouwenbergh, she wrote:

Bardstown, KY
Oct. 29, 1900

Dear mamma:

Sister Umberlin: [a nun at Bethlehem Academy, Bardstown] my teacher, told us to write a letter, so I am going to write to you. When are you and Uncle Joe[19] coming out? I hope cousin Beck will son [sic] be well enough for you to come. Laura Johnson was staying at Mrs. Henry Whelan's, so, now she is staying with us. Rebecca is still saying that she is home-sick and coming home. But I think she is putting on and acts silly. It makes me mad for her to do it.[20] Saturday we put the side saddle on Charlie, and went to look at the snares. I was in front and Ben was behind me. Coming back Charlie buck jumped; and threw us off. My foot was hung in the stirrup with my head nearly touching the ground, and there I was hanging with Charlie buck jumping. I couldn't see what had become of Ben. So when we got up Ben's nose was bleeding, and he was crying. The skin is off of his nose, and it is two or three times as large as ordinary. My head was hurt on top. I think I will not go on Charlie any more. How are you all? Much love to you all.

Your grand-child,
Nannie[21]

Even at the tender age of eleven Nancy demonstrated her fearlessness in danger, her strong will power, and her prudence. It was no wonder that she was her formidable father's favorite child. Nancy was so much like him.

A scant seven months after this incident, young Ben, not yet ten years old, died of complications from pneumonia, despite all the efforts of the family's doctors. The grieving family buried their youngest child in Saint Joseph's Cemetery less than half a mile from their home.

Little Ben's passing had a profound effect on Nannie. Always a sensitive and high-strung child, she was shocked by the suddenness of her brother's death and horrified by its utter finality. At the same time, the melodramatic Victorian rituals and trappings of mourning fascinated her. In her later life, Nancy tended to dramatize death to the extent that she thought it was important for the whole family to gather around the bedside of the dying member in order to hear the loved one's last words. She believed that the dying must speak to the living and say something either profound or sentimental. It greatly upset Nancy if this scenario failed to happen.

This first rent in the fabric of her family's protective cocoon rudely shook Nancy's sense of security. From then on, the young girl believed that death was an insatiable predator that lurked around every corner. This exaggerated fear and horror of mortality haunted her throughout the rest of her life.

Despite this family tragedy, the daily routines of school and play continued for Rebecca, Nannie, and Hendy. The three sisters received their primary education at Bethlehem Academy, a Catholic girls' school in Bardstown, and their secondary schooling at Loretto Academy. Founded in 1812 by the Lorettine Religious Sisters, the Loretto Academy's original mission was to provide an education for the daughters of Kentucky's frontier families.[22] While a teenager, Annie Kouwenbergh Johnson had studied there for four years, and she cherished the experience. She always believed that her academic and religious training had given her the well-rounded education that had molded her into the perfect helpmate for her ambitious husband. She wanted no less for her daughters.

Dreadfully homesick, Rebecca had attended the boarding school for less than three months before she persuaded her parents to allow her to return to her "own dear little home."[23] The youngest daughter, Hendy, also spent an abbreviated time at Loretto before her abundance of high spirits and mischievous pranks sent her back to Bardstown. Rebecca and Hendy completed their formal education as day students at nearby Nazareth Academy.

Nannie Crow Johnson, age twelve, enrolled at Loretto in the autumn of 1901. She, too, experienced a rocky start during her first month living away from home.

Loretto Academy,
Sept. 5, 1901

Dear mother and father:

Father Riley gave me the basket you sent; and I was so glad to get it. I have not been very home-sick. I cried some the first day; but the next morning I was feeling fine, until late that evening I cried; I have not cried since. Annie Bowling is coming Monday. Father Riley said he thought you were coming over here next week; I hope you are. Do not expect a letter from me on Thursday any more, because we are going to write on Sunday.

What teachers are at Bethlehem school now?

Tell Rebecca that Wilfrid [sic] came yesterday. There are so many new scholars this year. We are going to study Latin this year. There was a girl in my class that had been crying and wanting to go home, who turned up in the infirmary this morning sick. When y [sic] send my slumber slippers please send me a wash-rag too. I have not cried in bed since I've been here. Netty O'Brien sleeps next to me, and she has to wake me up every morning. Father, if mother comes next week, you try to come to [crossed out] with her. How is Hendy getting along at school?[24] I guess Rebecca will start to school Monday.[25] We have have [sic] been having a fine time. Sr. Rosine let us off from scool [crossed out] school two evenings and we went after grapes. When is Lizzie going home? Much love to you all. I have not heard from Stewart yet.

Your loving daughter,
Nannie.[26]

This letter marks one of the last times that Nancy signed her name as Nannie. When she turned thirteen in November, she decided to reinvent herself. She had always considered both the names "Nannie" and "Crow" to be undignified, but up until now she had lacked the courage or the confidence to change her identity. Now that she was away from parental influence, in new surroundings and making new friends, Nancy believed it was time to assume a more mature personality. For the next few years, she was known as merely "Nan." However, by the time she graduated in 1906, she was "Nancy Johnson." She had entirely dropped her middle name, Crow. Once she had shed her birth names, she never looked back. Though her name change was never formalized in a court of law, she would be known forever afterward as Nancy.

Nancy attended Loretto for the next five school years. Like her mother before her, she thrived under the strict discipline of the nuns and excelled in her studies. Every June on Commencement Day, she was awarded the coveted First Prize pin for scholarship. Dressed in her navy blue middy-style uniform and black high-button shoes, Nancy pursued a scholastic regime that emphasized literature, grammar, history, spelling, science, and mathematics; mathematics was her particular forte. The more "feminine" pursuits of drawing, music, and sewing held little attraction for her.[27]

As Nancy matured into a young woman, more of her father's personality traits emerged. Strong-willed and stubborn in the mold of Ben Johnson, Nancy believed that she could accomplish anything by sheer will power if she set her mind to it. In addition to her keen intellect, Nancy inherited her father's quick temper. Though she did not carry a pistol in her pocket as did her parents, Nancy learned to use her words with razor-sharp effectiveness. If her eloquence, wit, and will power did not achieve what she wanted, Nancy made use of another one of Ben's many tactics. Both father and daughter could cry real tears instantly and on cue. Since childhood, Nancy had become accustomed to getting her own way.

Nancy's positive traits included a deep devotion to her family and fierce loyalty to all those she loved. Once she formed a friendship, it was for life as far as Nancy was concerned. She saw no need to surround herself with crowds

Nancy Johnson in her school uniform at Loretto Academy, Loretto, Kentucky, circa 1905

of casual acquaintances; she placed her wholehearted trust in a select few people. As a friend, she was witty, charming, and full of gaiety.

On the other hand, Nancy did not mind having a few enemies. "It shows that you've got some character," she explained to her grandchildren, echoing Ben Johnson's own sentiments. Her father reveled in his political foes.

Seventeen-year-old Nancy Johnson graduated from Loretto on June 12, 1906, as her class's valedictorian. Her parents, particularly her father, were extremely proud of their most talented and now very attractive daughter.

During her last year at school, Nancy had blossomed into a dark-haired, gray-eyed beauty, resembling the models made famous by the artist Charles Dana Gibson.

The completion of Nancy's formal schooling came just in time. In November 1906, Ben Johnson was elected to serve as the representative of Kentucky's Fourth District in the U.S. House of Representatives. Following Christmas at their home in Bardstown, Annie Johnson and her daughters packed their bags and trunks with a plethora of new finery, and the family embarked for Washington, D.C. This phase of the Johnson family's life would continue for the next twenty years.

Washington, D.C., in the early 1900s was more like a small, sleepy southern town than the capital city of a growing world power. The social elite of New York, Boston, and Philadelphia looked down their collective noses at the brash politicians who strolled Washington's dusty streets and patronized the city's numerous bars and brothels. The aristocrats of New York's Fifth Avenue considered the Federal City to be a social backwater. "America was the only country in the world where having been born in a log cabin could be construed as a political advantage,"[28] but to the Johnson family of tiny Bardstown, Washington seemed like this side of paradise.

Once settled in their rooms at the Cochran Hotel on the corner of K and Fourteenth streets, Annie, with her daughters Rebecca and Nancy, dove into Washington's social whirl. Hendy, who was still a schoolgirl in 1907, was enrolled at Georgetown Visitation Academy, a prominent Catholic girls' school west of the city. The Johnsons soon discovered that the Washington upper crust divided itself into two distinct social groups: the congressional set that changed every two years, and the old, established families who had seen every presidential administration since Abigail Adams first hung up her wet laundry in the East Room of the newly completed White House.

Washington's native residents, known informally as "the cave dwellers," preferred that their little city's social scene be sedate. These Washingtonians considered anyone employed by the federal government, including the president of the United States, to be "too gauche for words."[29] However, Nancy Johnson, who was fresh from a country boarding school and hungry for excitement, found Washington to be a delightful round of theater box parties, afternoon teas, smart luncheons, card parties, White House receptions, charity balls, and, most especially, the wonderful "hops" at the U.S. Naval Academy in nearby Annapolis, Maryland. Closer to home, the Washington Barracks provided many handsome young army officers to squire the young women to picnics, baseball games, and dances.

Nancy Johnson of Bardstown, Kentucky, belle of Washington, D.C., society, circa 1909

One of Nancy's favorite pastimes was dancing, and she was quite proud of her skill, even seventy years later. Her graceful footwork was not only admired by her lucky partners but also reaped glowing compliments in the society columns of the Washington newspapers. "Miss Nancy Johnson won laurels by the beauty and the intricacy of her execution of the fashionable 'barn dance.' Her prowess is pre-eminent."[30]

Washington may have been a small town in the eyes of the world, but it did boast of several playhouses. Other than student theatricals of her Loretto days, Nancy had never seen a real play. Once in Washington, she became a devotee of the theater. Her favorite form of entertainment was the "musical plays," especially those written by the talented team of Henry Blossom and Victor Herbert. During her first three years in the nation's capital city, Nancy attended the "New National Theatre" at least once a month. Based on the programs that she saved, *The Red Mill* was her favorite production. Starring the famous comedy duo of David Montgomery and Fred A. Stone, the play was a hilarious farce about two Americans "doing" Europe, and who wind up in Katawyk-aan-Zee, Holland, at the Red Mill Inn. Nancy saw it on January 13, 1908, and again on January 25, 1909.

Nancy not only enjoyed seeing the plays but also the whole theater-going experience. Once settled in her box seat, she savored the scent of her little nosegays of "superb violets" fresh from Blackstone's florist shop on Fourteenth and H streets that her thoughtful escorts always provided for her. Everyone knew that Nancy adored flowers as much as she loved candy. While she waited for the curtain to rise on the evening's performance, she would nibble on the delicious caramels made by Velati's Confectioners located nearby at 620 Ninth Street. There were always boxes of Velati's caramels or Guth's chocolate-covered cherries on hand in her room at the Cochran Hotel.[31]

Nancy never spoke directly to the press, as her elegant mother had taught her, but she adored the attention given to her by members of the fourth estate. She had the habit of clipping snippets about herself from the newspapers and pasting them in the scrapbook that she had started when she moved to Washington in 1907. Early in her society years, Nancy identified neither the newspapers nor the dates of the clippings.

Rebecca and Hendy each enjoyed a social season in Washington before they retreated into the comforts of wedlock. Rebecca married her father's protégé, Dan Talbott, on October 12, 1909. Hendy followed her sister to the altar exactly two years later when she married Charles Lee Hamilton, a graduate of Princeton and a Louisville lawyer, in September 1911. By the spring of 1912, when both of her sisters were settled back in Kentucky, Nancy reigned in Washington as the sole "Johnson Girl," a distinction she enjoyed.

Despite the number of beaux who escorted her about the city, the pretty Kentuckian was in no hurry to join her sisters in the role of wife and mother. Nancy knew that once a woman was married, her carefree days were over. Young society matrons were expected to behave responsibly and to maintain a rigid respectability, while all the young belles danced until dawn. "I was having too much fun," Nancy explained a half-century later. "I wanted to kick up my heels."

As his seniority grew in the House, Ben Johnson made increasing use of his access to the press, ensuring that his publicity was always favorable. He recognized the political asset of his pretty daughter, and Johnson shamelessly fed tidbits of Nancy's activities to the ever-hungry newspaper reporters, thus keeping his own name and position before the eyes of the general public, particularly those of his constituents in Nelson County. Now that Nancy was the sole unmarried Johnson daughter, her newspaper coverage more than doubled. Ben

Johnson made sure that no item about Nancy was considered too trivial for the newspapers.

> STRICKEN WITH APPENDICITIS—Miss Nancy Johnson, Daughter of Congressman, Must Undergo Operation. Washington, April 13—Miss Nancy Johnson, daughter of Representative Ben Johnson, was stricken with appendicitis Saturday night. Her condition yesterday was serious, but is improved to-day.
>
> The physicians say an operation will be necessary.[32]

There was no operation or appendicitis. A few days later, Nancy's illness cleared itself up. The Washington stringer for the *Louisville Courier-Journal* informed a presumably relieved public that

> HONOR FOR MISS JOHNSON—For two consecutive congresses[33] Kentucky has been gracefully represented on the staff of the D.A.R. Pages.[34] Miss Nancy Johnson, the pretty brunette daughter of Hon. and Mrs. Ben Johnson, enjoyed the distinction this season, an attractive figure flitting about the hall[35] on official errands, generally in a girlish white frock and a big black Merry Widow hat. Last year, her sister, Miss Rebecca Johnson, was a page. Miss Johnson has entirely recovered from threatened appendicitis. The popularity of the chic little Kentuckian was attested by the burdens of flowers emptied into her rooms at the Hotel Cochran during her illness.[36]

A year later, Daisy Fitzhugh Ayres,[37] the Washington society columnist for the *Louisville Courier Journal,* continued to compliment Nancy in Ayres's characteristic high-blown style: "Miss Nancy Johnson, [Mrs. Ben Johnson's] debutante daughter . . . is attracting much attention, for she is a beauty and had been a belle in Washington society last winter."[38]

Thanks to some backstage maneuvering, Ben Johnson arranged for his daughter to be selected as the sponsor of the SS *Kentuckian,* a steamship of the American-Hawaiian line that was to be launched at Sparrows Point, Maryland, on March 19, 1910. Elated by this publicity coup, Johnson pulled out all the stops. Nancy got a smart new outfit with an eye-catching hat. Her proud parents had commissioned her prelaunch portrait to be taken by Clinedinst Studios—a photograph that quickly made its way onto the pages of the *Baltimore Sun, Baltimore Star, Baltimore American, Washington Times, Washington Star, Louisville Times, Louisville Courier-Journal,* and *Bardstown Kentucky Standard.* Even the lofty *New York World,* the premiere newspaper for the elite social circles of the day, featured Nancy's photo and accomplishment, noting that invitations to the launching ceremony had been sent to many friends, both political as well as personal.

Nancy Johnson, sponsor of the SS *Kentuckian*, Baltimore,
March 19, 1910

The most florid—as well as the most detailed—account of Nancy's moment in the spotlight flowed from the breathless pen of the adoring Daisy
Fitzhugh Ayres for the *Louisville Courier Journal.*

CHRISTENING—MISS NANCY JOHNSON SENDS KENTUCKIAN TO WATER—
Washington, March 25—It's a good deal like being a bride, only more so,
when you are a pretty girl in the smartest of togs and you are christening
a great monster of a ship with all kinds of dimensions in all kinds of
directions.[39]

The congressional girl, of all others, who has most brilliantly been basking in the limelight within the last few days, has been Miss Nancy Johnson, the handsome young daughter of Hon. Ben Johnson, Representative from Bardstown, Ky.

Through Congressman Talbott of Maryland, the Maryland Steel Company and the American-Hawaiian Steamship Line invited the pretty lassie "who was bred in old Kentucky where the meadow grass is blue" to be sponsor for their new Pacific liner, the "Kentuckian," launched with great eclat [sic] at the steel works where it is being built, at Sparrow's Point, just twelve miles the other side of Baltimore. Everybody who was invited by the fair young heroine of the occasion and her parents, to make the triumphal progress on the special train put at her disposal by the ship's company, were on hand exuberantly in all their Easter rigging.

The great "Kentuckian," yet in embryo, painted orange, lay on the edge of the Chesapeake Bay, her nose projecting upon the land into a platform built for the special guests. Miss Johnson was a picture of girlish brunette beauty in a natty little white serge tailored suit, with short kilted skirt, short coat, high white kid boots, a large sailor hat with rose colored braid with wide black velvet band and huge corsage bouquet of violets and gardenias. One arm was burdened with a sheaf of American Beauties [roses] as tall as herself. She held the bottle of christening fluid in a braiding of red, white and blue ribbons. By a sentimental departure from tradition, the momentous flagon contained instead of the time honored champagne, a blend of two historic waters from the little sponsor's own home state, water from the spring on the Larue County farm where Abraham Lincoln was born, water from the place in Todd County where Jefferson Davis was born—a happy and auspicious union. The sponsor, burdened with her trophies, was escorted to the place of honor by Mr. Steadman Bent, representing the President of the American-Hawaiian Line. Mr. Steadman gallantly had his shirt to match in tint the rose color of Miss Johnson's smart hat. A pink carnation of the exact psychological tint bloomed upon the young gentleman's gray lapel.

At the witching hour of twelve [noon], the fair Kentuckian smote her sister Kentuckian a blow of fellowship upon her graceful bow. "I name thee the Kentuckian!" cried Miss Johnson as the beribboned bottle shivered in her grasp. Instantly a paean of triumph went up from a thousand whistles far and near, as the craft slid rhythmically from the ways into the broad water. People yelled themselves hoarse. There were wavings [sic], congratulations and applause and the thing was done. "Don't you feel like Mrs.

Taft,[40] Nancy?" a young chum asked the star of the affair, as a dozen cameras were leveled ruthlessly toward her.

In the "joiners' shop" amidst many interesting appurtenances of ship building a hundred and fifty guests sat down to a superb banquet. Miss Johnson was presented by Capt. Burnham, President of the shipping company, with a very elegant silver jewel casket appropriately inscribed. At the "bride's table" facetiously dubbed, the heroine of the hour was surrounded by a few especial friends, among them Mr. Wood, President of the Maryland Steel Company. A "flat car," very crude and unconventional, but all the jollier for that, conveyed the company later on a regular joy ride to the great steel works, where all sorts of fiery diabolical stunts were in progress,[41] and everybody separately said perfectly originally, as they were being conducted personally through burning plowshares and cataracts of sparks: "Isn't it exactly like Dante's Inferno!"[42]

Ben Johnson basked in the glow of his daughter's limelight. Nancy, thrilled by the length and breadth of her press coverage, clipped out all her newspaper stories and pasted them into the souvenir album that the American-Hawaiian Steamship Company had presented her. Twenty-one-year-old Nancy Johnson felt that she had reached her pinnacle of social success. Christening a huge steamship had been the most exciting experience of her life. She was sure that nothing else would ever equal it.

CHAPTER 2 | *Going to Europe*

When Ben Johnson's constituents reelected him for a third congressional term in 1912, he moved his family out of the Cochran Hotel, where they had resided since 1907. They signed a lease for an attractive apartment on S Street in the northwest section of Washington. With a garage now at his disposal, Ben Johnson lost no time in filling it. He purchased a car for his favorite daughter. Nancy's electric brougham was a wildly extravagant gift at that time for a twenty-four-year-old single woman.

Once in possession of her own automobile, Nancy became her father's chauffeur—the only "real" job that she ever held. For the next year and a half, every weekday at noon she drove her father to the U.S. Capitol. Oftentimes the Speaker of the House, James Beauchamp "Champ" Clark,[1] accompanied Ben Johnson—a fact that Johnson made sure the press learned.

BOYS FOREVER—"Champ" Clark and "Ben" Johnson Daily Companions. Friends of Champ Clark and his folks are always commiserating with them in the regret that the speaker's family is motorcar-less. The Speaker declined his perquisite of a Government automobile. He wanted nothing on Uncle Sam.

Fair Chauffeuse [*sic*]. "I'd like to know what I'd want with an automobile of my own," drawled Mr. Clark in his quizzical, characteristic way, "when I got a pretty girl to drive me to the Capitol every day in her own private car. Can any of you fellows beat that?"

The pretty girl who is so benign is Miss Nancy Johnson, daughter of Representative Ben Johnson, one of the distinctly brilliant and interesting men in congressional circles.

Miss Johnson, who is a recognized Washington beauty and a terpsichorean expert, tools with neatness and dispatch her own smart electric brougham, bearing her own monogram on the panel in crimson letters.

Nancy Johnson, the "fair chauffeuse" in her own electric brougham with her
monogram on the panel. Photograph taken by Roscoe Crawford before Nancy
left Washington, D.C., for her trip to Europe, May 1914

Now this fair chauffeuse has a regular job at the nooning [*sic*] hour
every weekday conveying two steady passengers to the Capitol, her father
and Speaker Clark. After picking up the first at home, she collects her second fare from the apartment house where he lives, on the adjacent block
below, in Sixteenth Street.

This pleasant system has been existing for several years. Miss Nancy
never fails, rain or shine.

In close daily companionship with these two wise and witty men, the
young girl has gained much knowledge and insight into affairs.[2]

"I didn't pay them much mind," Nancy confessed years later. "I had to pay
attention to the road."

Ben Johnson beamed with pride in Nancy and in the flattering publicity
for himself. As the close friend of Speaker "Champ" Clark, Ben moved into
higher political circles.

In November 1913, Nancy turned twenty-five without any outward sign
that she was ready to find a suitable husband and settle down. She was long

past her debutant years, and now in her midtwenties, she was considered borderline to spinsterhood. Her married sisters, both living back in Kentucky, had already produced three children between them, with a fourth child on the way.[3]

In the meantime, Annie Johnson had become the Kentucky state regent for the Daughters of the American Revolution (DAR), and this organization took more of her time away from home. Beginning in early 1914, after the family returned to Washington from the Christmas break in Bardstown, Annie embarked on a one-woman crusade for national recognition that John Fitch of Bardstown was the true inventor of the steamboat. Annie not only wanted the recognition but also for Congress to appropriate funds to build a suitable memorial for Fitch in Bardstown.

Nancy, after eight social seasons in Washington, with its endless round of "dressing, dining, dancing and leaving of calling cards,"[4] was becoming restless. She had no desire to return to school, but she needed something more to occupy her intelligent mind besides driving her father around the city. She gave a fleeting thought to entering the convent as a nun and becoming a teacher, but quickly dropped that idea. She knew she did not have the required amount of patience.

"I was born too early," Nancy remarked in the 1980s. "I would have done well in business." However, a woman of Nancy's social station was not expected to actually work for her living. She was expected to marry well, have children, and devote the rest of her life to entertaining her husband's associates as well as doing charitable works.

Nancy began to give serious consideration toward traveling to Europe, especially when so many of her friends had returned in the fall of 1913 filled with glowing reports about the sights, the shopping, the new experiences, and the food of the Old World, especially France.

However, when Nancy first suggested the idea of a trip to Europe, her parents were less than enthusiastic. None of the Johnson family had ever sailed across the ocean. On the other hand, Annie's father had emigrated from Holland as a young man. Though he chose to live in the United States, William Kouwenberg[5] remained in close touch with his older sister Maria Blaisse[6] and her extended family in Holland. On February 18, 1864, William had married Rebecca Cox,[7] and they settled in Bowling Green, Kentucky. Their eldest daughter, Annie Mary, was Nancy's mother. All the Johnson children and grandchildren called William "Papa." After his wife's death in 1922, William returned to Holland, where he died on May 19, 1930.

In the first decade of the twentieth century, some of Annie's "Dutch cousins" had visited their American relatives in Kentucky, and they invited Ben

Ben Johnson seated on the porch of his home in Bardstown, Kentucky

and Annie to visit them in Amsterdam. Though Annie would have loved to accept these invitations, she knew that Ben would never leave American soil, so she always politely declined.

Ben Johnson had no desire to travel outside the United States. In fact, he had very little desire to go beyond the borders of his beloved Kentucky except to Washington, D.C., or occasionally to New York City. The farthest west he had ever ventured was once to Taos, New Mexico, in July 1899, when he had accompanied Annie and their ailing son, Ben, to a convent there, in the fruitless hope that the dry desert air would alleviate his son's chronic respiratory illness.

Ben Johnson could not understand why any sensible American would want to inconvenience himself or herself with uncomfortable living conditions among a lot of "foreigners" overseas. Being a man of plain tastes in his diet, Ben entertained no desire to upset his stomach with strange food or to subject himself to all sorts of unexpected nasty experiences. Beautiful Kentucky was good enough for him.

Except for her years at Loretto Academy under the watchful eyes of the nuns, Nancy had never lived out of her parents' sight, much less traveled on her

Lieutenant Roscoe
Campbell Crawford,
U.S. Army Corps of
Engineers, West Point
Class of 1912. Nancy's
"unsuitable" suitor

own across an ocean. Despite Nancy's heart-wringing pleas to learn to speak French in Paris, Annie and Ben had said "no."

Then in early 1914, Nancy's attention was caught by a handsome, soft-spoken second lieutenant in the U.S. Army Corps of Engineers stationed at the Washington Barracks, now known as Fort McNair.

Roscoe Campbell Crawford was born in Bridgewater, Pennsylvania, on November 1, 1887. He was the second youngest of eleven children. His parents had emigrated from Northern Ireland. As a young man, when Nancy first met him, his hair was the same color as a brick, so his family called him "Brick." He graduated third in the 1912 class at the U.S. Military Academy at West Point, New York, where his classmates nicknamed him "Red"—a name he kept all his life.

Despite Roscoe's good looks, charm, and sterling grades, he had three strikes against him in the eyes of Nancy's concerned parents. Crawford was neither a Kentuckian nor a southerner; he was not a Catholic; and he came from a large working-class Scots-Irish family. Furthermore, his dark red hair confirmed his unfashionable Irish roots. In early 1914, when Nancy again mentioned that she would like to visit Europe during the summer, the elder Johnsons seized upon this idea as a means of separating the couple before the relationship grew too serious. A prolonged absence from Washington could "cure" Nancy of her undesirable infatuation with Lieutenant Crawford.

Also that spring, Annie and Ben were distracted by the arrival of the family's first grandson. Their eldest daughter, Rebecca, gave birth to little Ben Johnson Talbott on March 1, 1914. In addition, Ben planned to run yet again for another term in the House of Representatives. With the election looming in November 1914, Ben needed to do serious campaigning in Nelson County, Kentucky. He could not keep a watchful eye on his middle daughter in Washington.

Bowing to necessity, both parents gave their permission for Nancy to sail away from their secure nest—once they had found someone suitable to chaperon her. Several of the family's close friends, including the parents of Nancy's best chum, Margaret McChord,[8] had tentative plans to journey to France in the middle of July. The McChords graciously invited Nancy to join them. Then fate—and the State Department—stepped into the picture.

On April 28, 1914, B. Harvey Carroll Jr., a scholarly man from Houston, Texas, who was a cousin of Senator Morris Sheppard of Kentucky, was appointed the new U.S. consul in Venice.[9] He and his wife intended to sail for Italy in late May. Since Washington was a smaller city in those days, word of Carroll's appointment circulated quickly among the political community. When the Johnsons asked the Carrolls to allow their daughter to accompany them, the Carrolls agreed to chaperone her in Italy.

Annie Johnson then looked among her social set for an equally suitable traveling companion who would be near to Nancy's age—someone with travel experience who would keep their head-strong daughter amused and out of trouble. The answer lived just a step around the corner on Sixteenth Street. Ethel Norris, the daughter of a Justice Department attorney, William F. Norris, was outgoing, friendly, and an experienced traveler. Though Nancy did not know Ethel very well, Annie was sure that would not be a problem. The young women would have plenty of time to get to know one another on the journey.

With the date of Nancy's departure moved two months earlier than expected, the Johnson household in Washington erupted into a flurry of preparations and packing. Everyone, it seemed, had his or her own idea of what Nancy ought to do when she got to Europe. Her father, still not comfortable with the idea of his daughter traipsing around a foreign land, thought that

Nancy should join her Dutch relatives as soon as possible after she docked in Genoa, Italy. He would breathe much easier once he knew she was safe among the far-flung family's fold. In fact, Ben thought it would be best if Nancy spent her entire time in Europe with her cousins in The Hague.

Nancy's grandfather William Kouwenbergh concurred with this idea, and he wrote her an eight-page letter that was packed with advice, most of which was unsolicited.

May 23d 1914

Dear Nancy,

Yours just received.—That your plans are very indefinite I can understand: because your trip was so hurriedly and unexpectedly conceived and decided upon. However this ought not to discourage you.

1st you are going to Italy, under the protection and guidance of the American consul at Venice; that fact alone will make everything safe & sure for you as far as any place in Italy is concerned, for he will see to it that you are well provided for.

2d you want to stay there at least one month: that's right; not only is Venice the place to visit but you can easily from there ["out" crossed out] go to see such places as you would like to see. Besides that, there will be American tourists calling on the consul, and plenty of them will be glad, on the recommendation of the consul alone, to have you join their party.

3d Your Father is anxious for you to go to Holland as soon as possible. This I think is the key to the solution of every difficulty.—My opinion of the whole matter is this: you will arrive in Italy, I should say, about the 10th or 12th of June; by the time you stay there for a month you will be in the midst of summer, which is not a good time to be in Italy. So, unless matters are entirely pleasant and congenial to you, I would then take a train that takes you, without change of cars to Holland. Once there you are at home, I say home, because I know how much your Cousin Mary in The Hague[10] appreciates the friendly & elegant reception given her children; but even without that you will be more than welcome, not only at her home, but at the home of all of those whose addresses I have given you. The great mistake most of the Americans make is to want to see the whole of Europe in 3 or 4 months; now this is simply an impossibility. Better see one country in all its different aspects, than to pass your time in railroad travel, and get a glimpse and a peep only of some cities, spread out all over Europe.— The Hague is worth seeing, Amsterdam is worth seeing, but you cannot see them in 2 days as most Americans try to do; besides The Hague &

Amsterdam is [*sic*] not <u>everything</u> in Holland.—Well now, you have a
good chance to see Holland just as it is. Traveling & entertainment in
hotels is cheaper there than in America; and from Holland to Belgium is
but a short trek; Antwerp & Brussels are well worth seeing & things are
very, very cheap there, in fact cheaper than anywhere else in Europe. And
from Brussels to Paris is hardly calling it traveling.—Again if you are
bound to go to Switzerland, you can have a magnificent trip by way of the
Rhine. Now all these things can be arranged for you while you are keeping
at the same time your headquarters in The Hague. Of course at this distance, I do not feel like telling you: do this or do that.—The only thing I <u>do</u>
know is, that comfortable & pleasant quarters, and a <u>welcome stay</u> are
waiting for you, not only in The Hague, but with <u>all</u> your relations. You will
be there, everywhere in the heart of Holland, easy & convenient to go from
one place to the other. When you are at your cousin William's[11] you will
find a man, more than anxious to give you a sight of the beauties of the
country, far removed from cities.—When you are in Schiedam you will
find your cousin Hubert and his excellent little wife, Anna,[12] and a whole
flood of little ones, ready and anxious to give you pleasure. At The Hague
with Mary & her family as I have said already—but what is the use of saying more about it; except this: in Amsterdam you will find Alphonse &
Joseph with Stef & Dora[13] and their little ones, and also the half sisters of
Clemence & Hubert, all ready and anxious to make your visit pleasant
and happy.

When you come back from Holland, where you can stay as long as you
want, <u>not a week or a month,</u> but as long as you want, I want you to write
to me, and tell me, if I have promised you too much.—By <u>all</u> means come
back on the <u>"Rotterdam"</u>; there you will find Mr. Edixhoven of whom I
wrote you; just tell him you are my grand-daughter, but Clemence &
Hubert will attend to that, I know.

I do not think your Cousin Mary will go to Switzerland or anywhere
else this summer, because she will have her hands full with Clemence.[14]—
Believe me you will not interfere with her arrangements; as soon as you are
in Italy, write to her & give her your address, so that she can communicate
with you, and then you can make all arrangements for your visit to Holland, or if any of your relations will be in Switzerland she can so inform
you, & you can meet them at some designated place.—In one word: if you
want anything, write to Mary; if anything suits you, write to Mary; if anything doesn't suit you, write to Mary; in one word: always write to Mary,
at least until you get better acquainted with the other relations.—

I have written to all of them in Holland, and I am sure they anxiously
& pleasantly look for you.

With love & best wishes for you all
Sincerely
Papa

P.S. When you are in Rotterdam, which city is next door to Schiedam, and
but little farther from The Hague, you might go and take a look at a church,
built there by your uncle Adrian, who was a Jesuit; and if you meet any one
there that belonged to his new parish, or any one of his first charge of the
other Jesuit Church, ask them if they knew Father Kouwenbergh,[15] and
then let me know what they said. Will you do that?

P.S. I want to tell you, that if you make your headquarters while in Europe,
with your relations in Holland, you will save much money, and very much
trouble.—And also do I want to tell you, that you can stay in Holland as
long as you want.[16]

Nancy kept her grandfather's letter, but she also kept her own counsel. In
Holland, Nancy had a total of nine first cousins and cousins-in-law, with nineteen second cousins plus their children. She had absolutely no intention of
moving in with her multitudinous Dutch relations, whom she barely knew, for
the entire duration of her stay in Europe. She would visit her cousins in due
time—but first she would follow her own agenda. Primarily she wanted to live
in Paris for the winter, where she could really learn to speak French and could
absorb the enticing French culture.

For her part, Annie Johnson was ecstatic when she realized that Nancy
would be going first to Italy. Once there, her daughter could fulfill a dream of
Annie's—to have an audience with the pope in Rome. Perhaps Nancy could
even have the honor of receiving Holy Communion from the Holy Father's
hands. With this thrilling prospect in mind, Annie contacted Monsignor William Russell, pastor of Saint Patrick's Church in Washington, D.C., asking him
for a letter of introduction to the Vatican for Nancy.

Monsignor Russell was only too happy to oblige this request from an influ-
ential member of his flock:

St. Patrick's Rectory

Washington, D.C.
May 25, 1914
Rt. Rev. S. Tampieri D.D.,

45 Lungo Tevere Mellini,
Rome, Italy

My dear Monsignor Tampieri:

I take great pleasure in introducing Miss Nancy Johnson, who will be accompanied by Mr. and Mrs. R. M. [*sic*] Carroll and Miss Norris. Miss Johnson is a devout Catholic and the daughter of one of our most distinguished representatives in Congress, and a personal friend of the President.[17] Mr. Carroll is the United States Consul at Venice. May I ask you to obtain an audience with the Holy Father,[18] and if possible, to obtain for Miss Johnson, who is the only Catholic in the party, the privilege of receiving Holy Communion from the Holy Father Himself? She and her father will deeply appreciate this great honor and I assure you that I shall be as grateful as though you had obtained the same privilege for a sister. Mr. Johnson is one of my most devoted friends and I cannot do too much to show my appreciation.

With all good wishes,
Sincerely yours,
Wm. J. Russell[19]

Father Russell did not exaggerate. The Johnsons did indeed know President Woodrow Wilson and his family. Nancy was a good friend of the Wilson daughters, Eleanor and Margaret. She had enjoyed the new president's hospitality on January 13, 1914, at the annual White House reception that opened Washington's winter social season.[20] Even in the midst of preparing for her trip, Nancy had shopped for a wedding gift to mark the nuptials of the president's daughter Eleanor to William Gibbs McAdoo on May 7.[21]

On May 15, the president took a brief respite from his worries over the U.S. Army's landing at Vera Cruz, Mexico, to compose an open letter to the diplomatic and consular officers of the United States. Written on White House stationery, Wilson's letter commended Nancy to the attention of his diplomats in Europe:

The White House, Washington
May 15, 1914

Gentlemen:

This will introduce to you Miss Nancy Johnson, the daughter of Representative Ben Johnson of Kentucky, who expects to sojourn in Europe. I commend her to your courtesy, bespeaking for her every attention which you properly can show her.

THE WHITE HOUSE
WASHINGTON

May 15, 1914

Gentlemen:

This will introduce to you Miss Nancy
Johnson, the daughter of Representative Ben
Johnson of Kentucky, who expects to sojourn
in Europe.   I commend her to your courtesy,
bespeaking for her every attention which you
properly can show her.

Sincerely yours,

Woodrow Wilson

To the
        Diplomatic and Consular Officers
                of the United States.

President Woodrow Wilson's letter of introduction for Nancy Johnson,
May 15, 1914

Sincerely yours,
[signed] Woodrow Wilson
To the Diplomatic and Consular Officers[22]
Of the United States

The president's letter would prove exceedingly useful to Nancy in the troubled
summer ahead.

CHAPTER 3

Innocents Abroad

B. Harvey Carroll was anxious to reach his new posting as quickly as possible before the summer tourist season began. He booked passage on board a second-tier Italian Line ship, the SS *Verona.*[1] It was a small passenger ship built in Belfast, Northern Ireland, and had made its first voyage in May 1908. The *Verona* was 482 feet long and 58 feet wide, and displaced 8,886 tons. It had a single yellow funnel, two radio masts, and twin-screw engines with a speed of fourteen knots, or about 16.1 statute miles per hour. The ship was scheduled to sail from New York City on Wednesday, May 27. Nancy Johnson did not care that she would make her grand entrance to Europe on board a small, slow, unfashionable ship. She just wanted to leave Washington before her overprotective father changed his mind.

KENTUCKY BEAUTY OF CONGRESS SET SAILS FOR EXTENDED STAY IN ITALY— Miss Nancy Johnson, daughter of Representative Ben Johnson and Mrs. Johnson has gone with friends to Italy to be away for several months. She is one of the most popular and attractive members in the National Capital.[2]

As Nancy's date of departure grew closer, time seemed to fly faster. Despite the wealth of advice she had received, she still had no firm idea how many months she would stay in Europe. She promised her parents that she would watch every penny that she spent. Though the Johnsons were wealthy by 1914 standards, Ben required his children to be thrifty. When each of his daughters had reached her midteens, he gave her a bank account with her own bankbook to manage. Nancy took pride in her money sense, though she was always able to rationalize large expenditures—at least to herself. As long as her parents would send her money, Nancy planned to bask in the wonders of great cathedrals and the beautiful palaces of Europe, and, most especially, to enjoy the experience of independent living.

Not knowing the weather conditions or social events she would encounter during the coming months, Nancy packed for every contingency. Her trunks overflowed with day frocks for sightseeing, tea gowns for summer afternoon parties, evening gowns for formal dinners, and sensible woolen skirts and jackets for the autumn's cooler climes. Annie made sure that Nancy also packed the customary black suit to wear for her audience with the pope. There were formal wraps, shawls, several dozen pairs of gloves, and an equal number of lace-edged handkerchiefs—each one carefully wrapped in tissue paper. One suitcase contained nothing but shoes and dancing slippers. There were also several hatboxes as well as bags for silk stockings, garters, and a plethora of underclothing. By the time Nancy had snapped shut her little train case, her luggage totaled a staggering twenty-six pieces.

In the midst of all this packing, Annie Johnson and Mrs. Norris cohosted several farewell parties for their daughters in the Norris family home on Sixteenth Street since the Johnsons' apartment was too small to accommodate all of their friends who were eager to wish bon voyage to Nancy and Ethel. Among the parting gifts that Nancy received was a Kodak box camera and some film—something she would begin to use even before her ship set sail.

Nancy and Roscoe had one last date before her trip—an outing in Nancy's automobile into the nearby countryside. Nancy brought along her camera, and they took pictures of each other. Either because Nancy and Roscoe were not familiar with operating a camera or because of the emotions at play during this last meeting, the three pictures they took are either blurred or overexposed.

On the morning of May 26, Nancy and Ethel, accompanied by Nancy's twenty-six pieces of luggage and Ethel's similar number of bags, boarded the New York–bound train at Washington's Union Station. Five hours later they arrived in the middle of the bustling financial and social capital of the nation. New York City was suffering from an unseasonable heat wave. That day, the temperature in downtown Manhattan rose to eighty degrees. The *New York Times* noted that it was the hottest May 26 since 1882.[3] Nancy barely noticed the discomfort. She was in New York City for the first time in her life, and she savored every moment of her short time there. She also looked forward to meeting her chaperons, B. Harvey and Daisy Carroll, and she could hardly wait for the next morning to arrive.

Meanwhile Nancy and Ethel spent the afternoon sightseeing in New York accompanied by a friend of Ethel's family. That evening, before going to the theater, Nancy dashed off a hurried letter on their hotel stationery to her father, who was in Kentucky campaigning for his reelection. This letter, and the ones

Nancy Johnson and Ethel Norris aboard the SS *Verona,* May 27–June 9, 1914

that followed it, were peppered with her constant explanations of her expenses and her attempted thrift. Nancy found it very difficult to economize when there was so much to see, to do, and to buy.

Hotel Seymour
Fifty West Forty-fifth Street
New York

My dear Father

Ethel and I got in to New York this afternoon and have been shopping and seen lots of the town. A very nice young man, a friend of Ethel's, met us at the station and has been taking us around and to-night will take us to the theatre.

Mrs. Shepperd [*sic*] came up to see the Carrolls off and are here at the Seymour with us. Ethel and I have the ["much" crossed out] nicest rooms with bath. Much too nice, but it is only for a day, which is six dollars, three dollars apiece and meals will not be much besides.[4]

Dr. and Mrs. B. Harvey
Carroll aboard the SS *Verona*,
May/June 1914. Dr. Carroll
was the new U.S. consul in
Venice, Italy.

How did you and little Rebecca[5] get along? Mother is going to stay at
McChords I think to night. They brought us up to the station and we had
quite a sad parting in tears, but I feel fine now and know we are going to
have a lovely trip. For two weeks our address at Genoa will be care American Consul General and later at Venice care American Consul. Give my love
to every body [*sic*] at Louisville & Bardstown, & tell them to write to me.

Love from Nancy

Postmarked "Times Square Station, NY. May 26 9:30 PM, 1914"[6]

May 27 dawned humid and overcast. The temperature climbed to the previous day's high as Nancy, Ethel, and the Carrolls walked up the gangway of
the *Verona*. A mountain of flowers greeted the excited young women when
they opened their stateroom door.

Once again, the *Louisville Courier-Journal*'s Washington society reporter,
Daisy Fitzhugh Ayres, recorded the event with a flowery pen, although this

time the intrepid reporter was not on the scene in New York City. Ayres got her details from Ben Johnson, who was also not present. However, a lack of eye-witness testimony never got in the way of a good story.

SAILS FOR VENICE—Washington, May 30—Miss Nancy Johnson is off on an idyllic trip. She threatens to be away for a solid year. But we really can't spare her that long.

On Wednesday at 11 o'clock, on the ship Verona, Italian Line, the beautiful young daughter of the chairman of the House District Committee sailed to spend the summer in Venice, going first to Genoa for ten days. She is with the newly-appointed United States Consul to Venice, Dr. H. B. Carroll [sic], of Houston, Tex., and his wife. Dr. Carroll, a very bright and scholarly man, is a cousin of Senator Morris Sheppard of Texas.

Another member of the party is Miss Ethel Norris, of Washington, a much-traveled girl, who is an intimate friend of Miss Johnson.[7] The two young ladies will be the guests of Dr. Carroll and Mrs. Carroll at a seashore cottage the consul and his wife will take for the summer in the city where the streets are paved with ripples.

Miss Johnson had been planning to go to Europe later in the summer with other friends when this earlier opportunity came to her.

A large part of her foreign absence will be spent with her mother's kins-people [sic], the Martens and the Braisses, who live in Holland. Miss Johnson expects to join these relatives in Switzerland and France, where they usually spend the summer, and return to Holland with them.

President Wilson and other dignitaries have provided personal letters to the young Kentuckian. When in Rome she will be presented to the Pope by a former papal delegate to Washington who is now a member of the College of Cardinals.

Miss Nancy Johnson is one of the prettiest and sweetest girls in Washington. You would realize this is not the mere opinion of a prejudiced Kentucky pen could you have seen the floral avalanche her stateroom on the Verona presented on Wednesday.[8]

When the all-ashore bell rang, the young travelers exchanged last-minute hugs and hurried kisses with their well-wishers, with promises to write often. Ethel and Nancy waved farewell to their loved ones, and to America, from the high deck of their ship. With a long blast of its horn, the Verona slipped its moorings, backed out of its berth, and began the two-week voyage across the Atlantic to Genoa. If Nancy felt a little misty-eyed, she did not admit it—not even to herself. She was on her way to independence. As the ship passed the

Statue of Liberty on Ellis Island, Nancy took a photograph of the famous land-
mark with her new camera.[9]

There was no hint on that warm noontime that any serious trouble was
brewing across the ocean. The headlines of the *New York Times* focused on
Western Hemisphere issues: "Mexican Problem Near Solution."[10] The lead
story on the front page reported the smooth progress of the peace negotiations, which had taken place at Niagara Falls, Ontario, and would hopefully
restore order in Mexico and dispatch Pancho Villa to the hinterlands. On the
International News page, the stories were remarkably lightweight, given the
festering situation that simmered like an angry boil beneath the early summertime face of Europe. London's Scotland Yard had foiled a plot to shoot King
George's horse that had been entered in the upcoming derby at Epsom. The
mood in Berlin also appeared lighthearted. Prince Oscar, the kaiser's fifth son,
had finally been granted his father's permission to marry a mere countess.
True love had triumphed.[11] The French were happy to inform the world that
their famous actress, Sarah Bernhardt, was not suffering from a serious illness;
she had merely sprained her ankle while descending from her automobile.[12]

Viewed through the rosy glass of hindsight, the summer of 1914 seemed the
most splendid, golden summer of all. Never had the sun shone down with
such gentle rays. Never had the skies over Europe been so clear and blue. The
grass in the Alpine meadows of Switzerland had never been so lush and green.
The waters of the Austrian spas had never sparkled so brightly. Or so Europe
appeared in retrospect.

In actual fact, the early summer weather throughout most of Europe was
anything but ideal. On May 26, a tidal wave struck Nice, while a late snow fell
in southern France. Shivering in forty-four degree temperatures, Parisians put
aside their new spring frocks in favor of warmer overcoats. Heavy storms
surged across the Mediterranean Sea; an earthquake rocked Sicily.[13] It seemed
to be a very inauspicious moment for two young travelers to begin their Grand
Tour of Europe. Nor could Nancy Johnson and Ethel Norris envision that their
trip would end abruptly before autumn with a dash for safety back to America aboard another poky little Italian ship named the *Principe di Udine*.

Despite the weather and the rumors, Americans crossed the Atlantic in
droves during May and June. As soon as the eastern seaboard colleges released
their students, several thousand high-spirited young men headed straight for
the Continent, where they took walking tours in Germany or art lessons in
Paris. They studied the languages and savored the frothy local brews. Among
these cheerful collegians was Arno Behnke,[14] a sophomore from Dartmouth
College in Hanover, New Hampshire, who hailed from Grand Rapids, Michigan. A member of the class of 1916, he was an enthusiastic participant in college

Arno Behnke, class of 1916, Dartmouth College, was a passenger aboard the *Principe di Udine* with Nancy Johnson. He later wrote a book about their journey back to New York entitled *The Sailing of a Refugee Ship*. Photograph courtesy of Dartmouth College Library

life, including his membership in the Delta Kappa Epsilon fraternity. In the summer of 1914, Behnke was twenty-one years of age. He planned to spend his vacation in the Swiss Alps. He had no idea that before his fall classes began at Dartmouth, he would have experienced the adventure of his lifetime and written a small book about it, entitled *Sailing of a Refugee Ship*, in which he chronicled the voyage and passengers of the *Principe di Udine* from Genoa to New York in August 1914.[15]

Professors also abandoned their books and boarded steamers to investigate once again the delights of the Old World. One of the future passengers of the *Principe di Udine* was Nicholas Butler,[16] the eminent president of Columbia University, together with his wife, Kate,[17] and daughter Sarah. In mid-June, without a care in the world, the Butler family sailed from New York to Le Havre, France. From there, they traveled first to Paris, and they planned to spend the month of August on a leisurely motorcar trip through northern Italy.

Throughout June and July, the great and the gracious, particularly members of the super-rich Vanderbilt family, crisscrossed the Continent. Among the vacationers were two of the most important future *Udine* passengers, the intensely private Frederick and Louise Vanderbilt,[18] who embarked on their annual holiday in the Southern Alps in early July. Frederick was one of the grandsons of the legendary Cornelius Vanderbilt, aka "the Commodore," who

Frederick and Louise Vanderbilt traveling in the Alps, summer 1914. Frederick
Vanderbilt is pictured outside the car, in the light overcoat. Louise Vanderbilt is
in the right-hand front seat. Photograph courtesy of the Roosevelt-Vanderbilt
National Historical Sites, National Park Services, Hyde Park, New York

Frederick Vanderbilt visiting the Pordoi Pass in northern Italy. This photograph
is captioned "The Boss." Summer 1914. Photograph courtesy of the Roosevelt-
Vanderbilt National Historical Sites, National Park Service, Hyde Park, New York

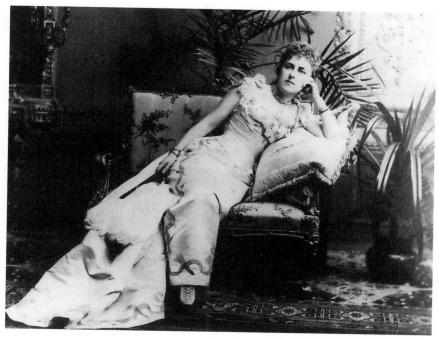

Louise "Lulu" Vanderbilt, circa 1890. Courtesy of the Roosevelt-Vanderbilt National Historical Sites, National Park Service, Hyde Park, New York

had founded the family's fortune in shipping and railroads. One of the few members of his famous family who did not squander his wealth in pursuit of ostentation, Frederick was the only family member of his generation to attend college, graduating from Yale in 1878. He began his employment in the offices of his father's railroad, the New York Central. Eventually Frederick became a director of twenty-two railroads. Though his family name was known for its staggering wealth, Frederick preferred to remain unknown to the general public. During his lifetime, he gave millions of dollars to philanthropy, but he tried to avoid any personal public connection with his benefactions. A sportsman like his brothers, Frederick also had a passion for yachting.[19]

In 1878, at the beginning of his final semester at Yale, Frederick eloped with Louise "Lulu" Anthony Torrance, a woman who was twelve years his senior and who had recently divorced one of Frederick's cousins. This marriage was probably the only rash thing that Frederick ever did. Initially the Vanderbilt family disapproved of the match, but Lulu's winning ways eventually captivated them. Lulu loved society and entertaining, though her shy husband did

not. Nevertheless their marriage was one of the happiest among the Vanderbilt clan.[20]

Usually the Vanderbilts spent the months of July and August cruising on
their yacht around the Mediterranean. This year, however, was different. In
January 1914, while on a pleasure cruise with several friends, the Vanderbilt's
boat, the *Warrior,* had run aground on a coral reef off the coast of Colombia.

Besides the Vanderbilts, the Duke and Duchess of Manchester and Lord
Arthur George Keith-Falconer were on board, reported an article in the *New
York Times*. "Lashed to the [ship's] rails and doubtful of being rescued during heavy seas, they watched eight lifeboats of the United Fruit Line *Fruitera*
smashed against the side of the ship in efforts to get a boat overside [*sic*] to rescue those on the Warrior. Another United Fruit boat finally effected the rescue
after the seas had calmed somewhat."[21] Following this harrowing experience,
Frederick decided to give up yachting. He sold the *Warrior* in May. In July 1914,
the Vanderbilts sailed to Europe aboard a commercial passenger liner.

Another important passenger on the future voyage of the *Udine* was Robert
A. C. Smith,[22] the energetic dock commissioner of New York City who annu-
ally returned to his birthplace in Devon, England, during the summer months.
The year 1914 was no exception. The family pilgrimage was an excellent opportunity for his daughter, Margaret, to visit her English cousins before the Smith
family moved on to tour the Continent. Smith, known as "RAC," was a man
of many diverse abilities. British by birth, he had been raised and educated in
Cadiz, Spain, and thus spoke fluent Spanish. This talent led to his first job as a
dealer in railway supplies for Cuba and other Latin American countries. RAC
Smith played as hard as he worked. An ardent yachtsman, he owned a sleek
boat and was an active member of several prestigious yacht clubs, including
the New York Yacht Club.[23]

Besides the rich, the powerful, and the famous, other Americans of more
modest means also visited Europe that summer of 1914. An estimated thirty
thousand midwestern schoolteachers took guided tours of the Continent. Most
of them were young women with thin pocketbooks who had saved nickels and
dimes for the opportunity to visit the places they taught about in their class-
room geography lessons. Also, several companies of the popular Wild West
shows crossed the Atlantic to present their unique, all-American brand of
entertainment to the appreciative Europeans. Among the actors of one show
were several dozen young men from the Onondaga tribe located in upstate
New York.

Quality folk and the merely moneyed; college professors and midwestern
schoolmarms; doctors, lawyers, and even Indian chiefs—all of them journeyed

to the Old World in 1914 for business or for pleasure. Everyone, like Nancy Johnson and Ethel Norris, looked forward to having a wonderful summer abroad. None of them expected the catastrophe in August that would mar their holidays and change the world forever.

Aboard the *Verona*, Nancy was delighted to discover that she was a good sailor. After an initial bout of seasickness, she and Ethel experienced two weeks of sun and warm sea breezes as the ship steamed across the Atlantic toward the Mediterranean. For the first part of the voyage, Nancy reveled in the luxury of sailing first class aboard an oceangoing steamer. She loved all the attention that a pretty, young, single woman attracted among the ship's officers and gentlemen passengers. One of her tablemates was the most interesting woman that Nancy had ever met. Marguerite Roby, a British subject, was an adventurous writer who had cycled through Africa accompanied only by Thomas, her native guide, as well as several bearers. Roby wrote of her experiences in a book titled *My Adventures in the Congo,* which was published in 1911.[24] In her letters home, Nancy expressed proper dismay at this most unconventional woman, but that was probably more for the benefit of her parents. Nancy envied Roby's independence and worldliness.

Nancy also learned more of the personality quirks of her companion. Ethel, supposedly the seasoned traveler, suffered long bouts of seasickness and homesickness in equal measure. Then, when Ethel felt better, she enjoyed listening to massive doses of grand opera, performed by a professional opera singer on board the *Verona*. Opera was not Nancy's favorite type of music; she much preferred the sprightly popular tunes of the era. Most of all, Nancy found herself resenting any special attention that Ethel might attract for herself. With her personal letter of introduction from President Wilson, Nancy considered herself the more important person of the two young women. This competition for attention would surface occasionally during the next few months.

During the second week at sea, boredom and a pang of guilt sent Nancy to her writing table, where she penned a long, episodic letter to her anxious parents in Washington.[25]

Navigazione, Generale Italiana

My dear Father and Mother

This is the tenth day out [June 5, 1914]. I have put off writing anything until now. And to-day has been so interesting I was afraid even then that I could only get in a little while, but now I have several hours. We do not get to Genoa until the eighth, which will make it fourteen days out. We do go

5.-

NAVIGAZIONE GENERALE ITALIANA

...was out bright and it all gave me the most mysterious feeling! I had Dr. Carrol relate to me some of the ancient history connected with these waters and countries, and I was carried back for generations. Morocco, Tangiers are cultured and civilized but they say about ten miles back is wild and barbarous as it was ten thousand years ago. To day we passed along the shores of Spain and saw the mountains of the Sierra Nevada, and back

Nancy's letter on stationery from the SS *Verona*, Navigazione Generale Italiana, June 5, 1914 by Naples first though, and Mrs. Carroll, Ethel and I were anxious to get off there and stay a week and take the next steamer. Then we could go to Pompeii, which is only a short distance but Dr. Carroll has to go on, and he says we can do as we like but he would rather we went on with him. Both he and Mrs. Carroll are lovely. We could not have found a better way to come and I am sure we are going to have a most wonderful time. I have been home sick so very little that really I could not call it that. I thought one day we were going to have a time with Ethel. She wept her heart out. There is a grand opera singer on board and she sang some of Ethel's operas that touched her emotions, and made her wish to be seated at her own little piano at home with Mother, but she soon got over it and has been well since. She was not very well at the time and at dinner some of "them furriners"[26] had been laughing at the way we ate, especially Ethel, or rather didn't eat as you ought to see the mixtures of spaget [sic][27] and every other imaginable thing with a little cheese that they put before us. We are the only Americans on board, and are really the whole show. The Captain is my old chum. I am teacher's pet. We play bridge every evening. The funniest thing is what a good game he plays and [he] knows only a very few words in English. But we get along just the same, Ethel with her Spanish can make herself understood. So can Dr. Carroll and Mrs. Carroll is studying all the time and soon I will in self defense. There is a little man, Italian from Chicago, who seems to be well educated and speaks English fluently, and he is my beau—or rather followed around like a little poodle until they all teased me and made so much fun of him to his face that now he rather lets me alone. But any way [sic] one day after dinner I was almost in tears, seasick to begin with and starved to death, and could not eat a thing they had put before me, so I confided to him, and the Captain came up and he told him and the dear Captain sent for the head waiter and told him to have cooked any thing I ordered any time and all he could think of was roast beef Americano, so they have served that to us at all times, especially cooked with little brown potatoes, but minus all the garlic and tomatoes and spaghetti that they season every thing with. The table is really wonderful and sometimes they have things that I really like. The cakes and ices and pastries are delicious and that with the fruits, oranges, apples, cherries, pears, figs, nuts, bananas save my life. They have fried brains in olive oil— they fry everything in olive oil—that look fine, but I can not eat brains and mushrooms, egg plant, asparagus which is fine, and a consume soup that makes me sick to smell, because I ate it when I was sea sick with powdered cheese that they put in everything.[28] They have all kinds of wine, and strange I can not drink it. Have lost all taste for it. They drink it instead of water. Poor Dr. Carroll has been sick from the time we left New York almost until to-day. The sea is perfectly smooth now. I had really only one bad day. I vomited a good many times, but it wasn't so bad, soon that is all over and the next day I stayed in bed as a precaution. The sea got very rough. We were going through the Gulf Stream just south of New Foundland [sic], and it was very, very windy and cold. The Captain got telegrams warning him of ice bergs, which were about sixty miles to the north, but that made it very cold. One night the captain was worried because of ice bergs.[29] Of course we all sit at the Captain's table. [Page three is missing.] . . . the Mediterranean we will have them all about us.

My letter was iterrupted [sic] here to have tea. And my friend came in to have it with me. He had been talking to the Captain and the captain said I was the finest English girl that had been on the ship since he had been on. Ethel and I are the only girls on. It is nice to be on a small steamer and be the whole thing.[30] They think Dr. Carroll something big of course and we get all the attention we want.

Then there is the strangest woman on board, Marguerite Roby a writer. She has been to all parts of the world, into the innermost parts of Africa and written her experiences. She is the weirdest looking thing, smokes cigarettes and drinks and has letters from all the kings of Europe commending her work. But every one laughs at her, and has nothing to do with her/Much [sic].

There is so much to write that I cannot get it all in the right places and I am interrupted so many times.

This morning the sea was alive with whales, they would come up out of the water all around us. Our trunks will be sent by freighter on to Venice. I would like to have them in Genoa but can get along. We have not been dressing on the boat, but will dress up for the Captain's dinner which is the evening before we land.[31] I really am learning a little Italian. I thought I would try to surprise you with it, but guess I will never know enough for that. But I will get some knowledge of it. I ["kn" crossed out] now have the pronunciation and the method Mrs. Carroll has is fine, which I will try to study. The voyage has almost made new persons out of us, if only you and Father could get round trip tickets which are <u>very reasonable</u> and cross on this slm [sic] boat just for the voyage. Round trip tickets are good for several months.

June 6—["Friday" crossed out] Sat.

Last night we passed the Straits of Gibralta [*sic*]![32] Dr. & Mrs. Carrol [*sic*] and I went up on the Captain's deck.[33] There was Africa on one side and Spain on the other. We passed between twelve and one [o'clock]. We were very, very close to Africa, and besides the lights could plainly see the dark shores rising high above the waters. The moon was out bright and it gave me the most mysterious feeling! I had Dr. Carrol [*sic*] relate to me some of the ancient history connected with these waters and centuries, and I was carried back for generations. Morocca [*sic*],[34] Tangiers are cultured and civilized but they say about ten miles back is wild and barbarous as it was two thousand years ago. To day [*sic*] we passed along the shores of Spain and saw the mountains of the Sierra Nevada, and back in the distance one high snow covered peak. To see all these places and countries brings it to me as real, like nothing else could do. The rocks of Gibraltar I never expected to see—and Africa I thought was just a myth. Africa and Europe are so near that one can stand on the shore of one and see the other. I will write a little more to morrow and mail it Monday at Naples. I do wish we could stay at Naples and go to Vesuvias [*sic*] and Pompeii. And I think maybe we will.

[Written in pencil] Monday—the eighth—4 o'clock

We land at Naples to-night at eight, and leave to morrow at twelve. Will be in Genoa and then go to Venice and will be at first at Hotel Brittanica [*sic*], Venice, care American Consul—Do write me often and tell me all about little Rebecca & all. I will write once a week—every Sunday will mail it, as it costs five cents a letter. And we may get very hard up—We have been hearing Grand Opera since luncheon and I have not had any time to write.

Loads of love to you all. Tell Mrs. Norris not to worry, neither Ethel nor I has [*sic*] been homesick. Our trunks, the large ones will go on to Venice and we will get along the best we can in Genoa. So far we have been doing on very few clothes. We, Ethel and I will have to tip about five dollars apiece for the voyage. We give it to the head man to be distributed. Some will tip much more. Such service as we have gotten has been wonderful— chocolate, tea & cakes or anything brought in to us almost any time we wanted—

Do write me. Tell Margaret and Sally I will write them at Genoa.

Love, Nancy[35]

CHAPTER 4

The Powder Keg of Europe

"What's past is prologue," observed Shakespeare in *The Tempest,* an apt description of the events that took place during the first half of the twentieth century. The origins of the First World War could be traced back to the fall of the Roman Empire, but most historians prefer to keep it simple and begin with the Treaty of Frankfurt in 1871 that ended the Franco-Prussian War. Germany, the youngest nation in Europe, had defeated France, but it was a hollow victory. Though Germany received the spoils—the provinces of Alsace and Lorraine—Paris, not the German capital of Berlin, continued to be the center of culture, style, and beauty.

Nationalism—the identification with one's country rather than with one's village or clan—was a novel idea that swept through Europe during the nineteenth century. Shakespeare may have been the first Englishman to voice love for his country when he wrote young Henry V's battle cry, "On for England, Harry and Saint George!" By the 1880s, England glowed with pride in the British Empire upon which "the sun never set."

The French Revolution literally erased the last vestiges of the ancient feudal system in France, and it solidified the French people's passion for their country. "The Marseillaise," composed by Claude Joseph Rouget de Lisle in 1792, galvanized the ragtag peasantry into an army. Later the song became the French national anthem. The opening line, "Allons, enfants de la Patrie," took deep root in every French person's soul. Though defeated by the upstart Germans in 1871, the French never lost heart—or their urge to revenge this stain on their national honor.

The sleeping giant of Russia awoke with a start when its new railroad system crisscrossed that vast country, connecting the scattered, diverse population centers with one another. In a single generation, the bewildered peasants were pulled from the Middle Ages into the modern world. By the early 1900s, the growing discontent among the impoverished masses threatened to destroy the weakened aristocracy. Though the people professed their devotion for Mother Russia, the Revolution of 1904 showed how much they hated their oppressive government.

In Germany, an arrogant young peacock strutted into the spotlight. Prince Friederich Wilhelm Viktor Albert, heir to the throne of Prussia, was born in 1859.[1] His mother was Princess Victoria, eldest daughter of England's Queen Victoria. Wilhelm was first cousin to England's King George V as well as being related to most of Europe's royal families. He grew to manhood during the tumultuous era when his grandfather, Kaiser Wilhelm I, aided by his chancellor, Otto Von Bismarck, united the kingdoms of Germany. The young prince, handicapped from birth by a withered arm and unloved by his parents, longed to win universal approval and admiration for his strength and brilliance. Denied this affirmation by his cold, distant family, Wilhelm compensated for his monumental insecurities with nationalistic fervor. In 1888, at the age of twenty-nine, Wilhelm inherited the German Empire. It would soon become apparent that he was supremely the wrong man in the wrong place at the wrong time.

Immature despite his years and education, intelligent, impatient, quick-tempered, and disastrously impetuous, Kaiser Wilhelm II possessed all the traits of the classic bully. He was quick to perceive slights against him when none existed. His blustering, bragging, and occasionally cruel exterior masked his gnawing insecurities. Wilhelm believed in the divine right of kings, and he loved to wear military dress uniforms dripping with gold braid and decorations. A supreme egotist, he could never bring himself to acknowledge a mistake, especially when his impatience or his lack of tact had created one. This volatile mixture in Wilhelm's personality would prove deadly as the twentieth century dawned.

While the Great Powers of Europe—Germany, France, Russia, Austria-Hungary, and Great Britain—jockeyed for position, old hatreds festered and tensions grew. In the nineteenth century, Europe had enjoyed nearly a century of relative tranquility since Napoleon's defeat at Waterloo, except for the failed midcentury revolutions and the occasional spats among the always-fractious Balkans. Thomas Mann, the German novelist and a contemporary observer, noted that, owing to the boredom brought on by peace, many in Europe would welcome the idea of warfare.[2] The egocentric kaiser believed that it was Germany's destiny to dominate Europe.

In the early 1900s, Germany began a massive naval ship building program, ostensibly as a defense against possible aggression by other nations, but also as a means to expand its overseas empire. Huge warships called dreadnoughts, cruisers, and a fleet of submarines rolled down the ways of German shipyards.

Though the kaiser glowed with pride in his navy, he was deeply jealous of France. Above all else, he yearned to visit the beautiful city of Paris—Berlin's archrival. Twice Wilhelm had hinted to the French government that it should invite him to Paris, where the French could welcome him with honor and bestow more decorations for his uniforms. He pointed out that since Germany had won the war in 1871, his country should be given due respect. France ignored the kaiser's blatant suggestions. France's "slight" not only outraged Wilhelm personally, but it also solidified the kaiser's belief that Germany must be recognized as Europe's preeminent country. France, always perceived as a rival, now became the enemy—one that must be crushed so thoroughly that it could never again be recognized as a first-tier nation. This bellicose posturing of Germany naturally made the French very uneasy.

In 1911 General Friedrich von Bernhardi published a book entitled *Germany and the Next War.* "War is a biological necessity . . . the law of the struggle for existence," he wrote. Warming to his belligerent topic, the general explained that it was absolutely necessary for Germany to ensure its power "as befits our importance." This power was a "political necessity that must be *fought for.*" Conquest of foreign territories "thus becomes a law of necessity." Furthermore, Germany "must act on the offensive and strike the first blow. . . . France must be so completely crushed that she can never cross our path again."[3]

By 1914, Germany had become almost a military state. The general population of that country held the military in the highest esteem. Over the past thirty years, the ideology of Germany had changed from conservative to nationalistic and aggressive. "Materialism, bellicosity, the glorification of violence and war, worship of the naked *Macht* superseded the more reasonable, idealistic and humane elements in the German spirit."[4]

Caught amid these nations that juggled Europe's balance of power were their smaller neighbors: Holland, Luxembourg, Switzerland, Belgium, Italy, the Scandinavian countries, and Turkey—known as "the sick man of Europe"—as well as the always quarrelsome Balkans. With growing alarm, these countries watched Germany build up its army and munitions. In order to preserve the neutrality of these smaller countries, especially Belgium, which lay directly in the path between France and Germany, confusing, entangling, webs of alliances formed among the European nations that would bind them to their stronger neighbors in times of peril.

By the time of the death of England's King Edward VII in May 1910, it was a foregone conclusion that war between Germany and France was inevitable—

the only question remained: when? King Edward, known as "The Uncle of Europe," had been the fragile glue that kept Europe at peace. Marching in his funeral procession on May 20, 1910, were nine ruling monarchs, seven queens, five crown princes, and forty other members of Europe's royal families. It was the largest single gathering of royalty that anyone could remember—and it was also the last. Within five years, most of these rulers would be locked in deadly combat with each other in the greatest conflict the world had yet witnessed. Few monarchs would survive the Great War with their crowns still on their heads.

The long eastern border that Germany shared with Russia and the smaller, mountainous frontier with France made the Germans feel claustrophobic. The kaiser and his generals continually complained of encirclement. If war broke out and Russia allied with France, Germany would find itself fighting on two fronts. With this grim possibility in mind, more men were called up for the German army.

In the meantime, German engineers began dredging and widening the Kiel Canal between the Baltic and North seas to enable their warships to deploy to the open ocean more rapidly. The Kiel Canal was over sixty-one miles long and had originally been excavated between June 1887 and June 1895. It reduced the distance for passage between the Baltic and the North Sea by 280 nautical miles, or about one day. With the launching of the large dreadnoughts, the Kiel Canal needed to be deepened and widened.[5] England looked over its shoulder and shuddered. Britannia's superior sea power had ruled the waves since 1588, but now the island kingdom faced the possibility of a naval attack by Germany.

Attack was definitely the focus of the German leadership. As early as 1904, Count Alfred von Schlieffen,[6] chief of the German General Staff, had formulated a battle plan—a blueprint that he continued to refine until his retirement in 1906. Should Germany face a two-front war, "the whole of Germany must throw itself upon *one* enemy: the strongest, most powerful, most dangerous enemy, and that can only be France," he concluded.[7] Schlieffen allotted six weeks for the capture of Paris—the time he estimated it would take the ponderous Russian army to mobilize. Therefore, Schlieffen reasoned, it would be a "military necessity" to take the quickest route to France—straight through Belgium. He dismissed Belgium's recognized neutrality as a mere "difficulty." The kaiser and his government agreed. Belgium's subsequent fate in the coming war was sealed as early as 1907.

Meanwhile the French devised their own battle plan against their saber-rattling neighbor. While the Schlieffen outline for war was precise in detail, it lacked flexibility. France, on the other hand, relied upon the improvisational skills of its generals on the battlefield. The French plan also called for an offensive strategy, considering that the best defense is often a good offense. Consequently, while the Germans saw themselves marching toward Paris in an ever-widening arc around the right flank, the French created Plan 17—an attacking maneuver aimed straight at the enemy's center and left flank through the rough terrain of the Ardennes Mountains. Geography and history were against this plan. Centuries earlier, it had taken the disciplined Roman army of Julius Caesar ten days to hack their way through the region.

Nevertheless the French felt optimistic. What their army lacked in manpower or strategy, they would make up with their famed élan.

With the buildup of the German navy, Britain was forced to chart its own defense plans in the case of a full-scale war on the Continent. The British military establishment underwent a complete overhaul.

By March 1911, General Henry Wilson, the director of British Military Operations,[8] believed that England could mobilize its army by the fourth day of a German invasion of Belgium, the logical route into France. His three-point program was simple—on paper: join the French, mobilize the same day as the French, and use the entire British army to defend France. Wilson's civilian superiors were not impressed with his war jitters—except for one far-seeing young man in the cabinet—Home Secretary Winston Churchill[9] understood exactly what Wilson meant.

The thirty-seven-year-old Churchill chided his colleagues when few listened to Wilson in 1911. By 1913, Churchill had become the First Lord of the Admiralty, where he could now actually *do* something. By then, Germany's belligerent intentions had become apparent. At a meeting in the Admiralty on February 19, 1913, Churchill gave his opinion that Germany would invade Belgium in September 1914—by that time the dredging of the Kiel Canal would have been completed, and the harvest would have been gathered for the winter.

By the spring of 1914, the French army, inspired by the military theories of General Ferdinand Foch,[10] director of France's War College, had completed its reorganization. It now felt ready to respond immediately should Germany raise its sword against France.

In early 1914, the German army numbered 1.5 million men. American author Theodore Dreiser observed at firsthand Germany's preparations for war, even though war had not been declared. "Around the corner a full regiment suddenly came into view . . . their brass helmets glittering. Their trousers were gray and their jackets red and they marched with a slap, slap, slap of their feet that was positively ominous. Every man's body was as erect as a poker; every man's gun was carried with almost loving grace on his shoulder."[11]

The Kiel Canal upgrade was completed in June 1914, three months earlier than Churchill had anticipated. Citing the French military preparations near the border of his country as justification, the kaiser strengthened his military forces along Germany's frontiers. Despite his loud posturing, Kaiser Wilhelm honestly did not seek world domination through a major war. He thought that a quick victory over France would give Germany recognition as a major power and the world's respect that it deserved. Even better, he hoped to frighten France into submission without resorting to a real shooting war.

No one in Germany, especially the bankers, industrialists, and civilian ministers, expected that a conflict with their neighbors would last longer than three or four months. Because of the Great Powers' mutual economic interdependence, a prolonged war was unthinkable and therefore impossible.[12] Yet there were a few intelligent men in Germany who recognized the full implications of what would happen if they should light the powder keg under them. General Helmuth von Moltke,[13] who had succeeded General Schlieffen as chief of staff in 1906, warned the kaiser that a war would be not a quick battle, but a long, drawn-out campaign. Unfortunately the kaiser chose to ignore the prophecy of his top military adviser.

While the European nations eyed each other with growing distrust and rattled their half-drawn swords, the Americans had very little inkling of what was going on "over there"—nor did many people care. For the past fifty years, the United States had looked backward and inward on itself, first to the still-tender scars left by the American Civil War, then to the expansion into the western territories.

Since the 1870s, business had boomed on the western shore of the Atlantic. Ambitious men named Morgan, Astor, Carnegie, Rockefeller, and Vanderbilt earned huge fortunes in coal, steel, railroads, steamships, and other industrial ventures. For the families of these gifted few, diamonds, lavish mansions, yachts, and fantastic parties became a way of life.

"Society is an occupation in itself," remarked Ward McAllister to a reporter from the *New York Herald Tribune* in March 1888. "Only a man who has a good deal of leisure and a taste for it can keep up with its demands."[14]

In the United States of the 1890s, 90 percent of the country's wealth was controlled by 10 percent of the population.[15] Cushioned by their fortunes, the upper class became supremely and myopically self-indulgent. The pampered descendants of the robber barons were so insulated from the realities of the average American worker's life that the members of the upper class never had cause to doubt their own God-given right to their money and its attendant privileges. Money-in-hand bought material comforts, smooth service,

first place at the head of the line, and privacy on demand.[16] The grand expec-
tations of America's rich families were never more evident than when the
wealthy went on vacation in Old World Europe. And in 1914 more than one
hundred thousand Americans, many of them very wealthy, crossed the Atlantic
without a notion of what lay ahead on the other side. In their coddled innocence, they believed that their American citizenship and their money would
buy them all the comforts and personal security that they desired.

CHAPTER 5

The Fuse Is Lit

Nancy, Ethel, and the Carrolls were completely oblivious to the dark war clouds looming on Europe's horizon when they arrived in Naples on the balmy evening of June 9. There the party enjoyed their brief overnight visit in Naples before the *Verona* weighed anchor and steamed up the western coast of Italy to Genoa, finally arriving there on June 10. Expatriate American author Henry James described this ancient seaport as "the crookedest [*sic*] and most incoherent of cities, tossed about on the sides and crests of a dozen hills."[1] To the young woman from Bardstown, it was unlike any place that she had ever seen. Nancy was immediately enchanted by the exotic, ancient port.

Meeting the *Verona* was John Edward Jones,[2] the U.S. consul general in Italy. Born in the District of Columbia, Jones received his undergraduate degree from Georgetown University and his law degree from Columbia University in New York. He worked for the *Washington Star* newspaper for sixteen years before he entered the diplomatic service in 1906. Prior to his posting to Genoa, Italy, in 1913, Jones had served in such diverse places as Manchuria and Canada. Now he was a widower with three children.[3] The consul general was a handsome man, forty-five years of age, with slightly graying hair, clear eyes, and a ready smile. He possessed an optimistic, cheerful personality, and his empathetic nature made him a perfect fit for his job. From their first meeting, Nancy was quite charmed by him. In turn, Jones was equally pleased to welcome some fellow Washingtonians to Genoa, and he gave particular attention to the congressman's pretty daughter. Perhaps Nancy's letter of introduction from President Wilson had something to do with the extra warmth of Jones's cordial reception.

Also waiting for Nancy and Ethel were the long-expected letters from home. Nancy's envelope included a newspaper clipping of Daisy Fitzhugh Ayres's complimentary description of their departure from New York. Nancy was extremely pleased by Ayres's article, especially since it barely mentioned Ethel. After two weeks at sea in close quarters, Ethel's personality had begun to grate against Nancy's, particularly since Ethel seemed to make friends more easily than did Nancy. Like her father, Nancy wanted to be first in everyone's opinion—just as the flowing pen of Aeyrs's news stories had described her.

Before traveling on to Venice, the Carrolls and their charges stayed a few extra days in Genoa, soaking up new experiences. Ever the thoughtful host, Jones provided the party with the services of his vice consul, John B. Young, who was another native of Washington, D.C. First posted by the State Department to Milan in 1909, in 1914 Young was still a bachelor. An Italian staff member at the consulate, a Mr. Laugieri, who acted as the Carrolls' interpreter and courier, rounded out the group. Laugieri was young and handsome, and flattered the young women with his Italian charm. Nancy and Ethel commenced an unspoken tug-of-war for both men's attentions.

After settling into her room at Genoa's Eden Palace Hotel, Nancy wrote another long letter home, describing her exciting midnight supper in Naples and the sights of Genoa. One spot that intrigued Nancy was Campo Santo, one of Italy's most famous cemeteries. Situated on a hillside outside of Genoa and laid out in 1867, it is known for its ornamental monuments, magnificent statuary, and a domed rotunda near the top of the hill. The wealthy of Genoa are interred in marble vaults that surround a large quadrangle. Only the city's poor are buried in the ground.

In her letter, Nancy also made sure to emphasize her thrift, despite the fact that she was spending her allowance at an alarming rate. Inserted in her rush of news, she mentioned that she was not going directly to Holland and her cousin's home. This slip of the pen was entirely intentional. Now that she was safely in Italy and far from her parents' immediate influence, Nancy intended to exert her independence in the ticklish matter of her long-range travel plans.

Eden Palace Hotel
Parc Hotel
Genes [*sic*]

My dear Mother

    We have been in Genoa two days now and really we are having the most wonderful time. We got to Naples at eight o'clock and left at six in the morning but did not go to bed at all until the boat left. We surely made an all night of it that time. It was about half past nine before we landed and were ready to go up into town. My little Italian beau[4] was to take us around and show us the sights, but as he was going to get off there and stay, he was

To the Berlitz School. Tell Margaret to write me. I have not written to Papa or any of the others yet and instead of writing a long letter, if you would send this and my other letter to them, they would know something about what I am doing. Am glad they thought little Rebecca so sweet. Ethel and I went down to the Consul's office yesterday. Found him all alone, he was so proud. We must not be out after five o'clock by ourselves.

Nancy's letter written on stationery from the Eden Palace Hotel, Genoa, Italy, June 1914

so long in the Custom house that we did not wait but the four of us got the
carriage and rode all over town. It was fifty cents an hour for us or seventy-
five cents apiece for two hours. Carriage hire is the only cheap thing I have
found here. We got back to the boat a little before twelve and there met Mr.
Centorbi, the man who was going to take us out and he wanted us to go
then, so Dr. Carroll, Ethel & I went with him. We were anxious to stay up
and see the sunrise and our departure from the Bay of Naples any way. We
took another long ride, first took a Miss Jiana,[5] a Vassar school teacher, old
maid, to her hotel, and went to a famous restaurant, St. Lucia and had supper.[6] They brought out live lobsters which they then cooked for us, and I
have never tasted such sweet delicious meat in my life. The restaurant is
right on the bay where the lobsters are caught. It was over a foot long. Mr.
Centorbi paid for the supper which was five dollars.[7] We then went back to
the boat and played bridge until we left. Vesuvious [sic] was just a few miles
away and at present is smoking. The whole bay of Naples is considered the
most beautiful in the world and it was magnificent. There were five big
battleships in the bay. We got to Genoa and went to a very nice hotel, but
after Dr. Carrol [sic] had dressed all up and called upon Dr. Jones, the
American Consul General, he came back with the information that Dr.
Jones insisted upon us going to the Eden Palace Hotel where he lived. As
this is the most expensive hotel in town naturally we didn't like the idea
much as I have now to see a big hole coming in my pocket soon. At ten
o'clock, we all went to call on the General[8] and such a sight met our gaze.
Out tripped this gay widower in the Rogers style—wife only been dead a
year and now looking for another one to take care of his three children. He
is very rich and the best looking thing you ever saw. If Ethel or I we [sic]
don't catch him we are too slow. He has taken us every place. In fact already
adopted us. He got special suites for us here, two & a half apiece a day,[9]
which includes meals that are delicious. The hotel is an old castle with
beautiful old gardens & trees of all kinds with fruits, oranges, bananas and
some fruits I never saw before. Am enclosing a post card with our rooms
marked. Save it for me. Yesterday, we went out to this cemetery, Campa
Santo [sic], which is the famous cemetery. This long colonnade all of marble, with graves under it. Each family section is marked with magnificent
statuary, sometimes the [several words indecipherable]—made from life
and really a likeness of the people. It costs about two thousand dollars to
be buried there.[10]

    The Duke of the Abruzzi[11] has left and may return in a few days, if he
does, Dr. Jones is going to have us meet him. He says if we go to Rome he

will arrange to have us meet the King & Queen.[12] He seems to want to do everything for us. Dr. Carrol gave him his bottle of whiskey,[13] and I gave the other to the captain on the Verona. Our baggage was not examined at all. Just passed on through. Mrs. Carrol is very anxious for the whiskey, did not want Dr. Carrol to give it away. She wants it for sickness. If it would not cost too much to send, would like for Father to send a bottle to Mrs. Carrol. I was so glad to get your letter. I got yours as soon as we got to Genoa. Ethel got one from her mother that afternoon. Father Russell's letters came.[14] Do not forget to pay Clinedinst[15] for picture. It was nice of Julian[16] to wire me. I am afraid I will not want to leave to go to Holland.[17] It is almost time for Dr. Carroll and General Jones to come to lunch. Dr. Carroll has started to the Berlitz School.[18] Tell Margaret[19] to write me. I have not written to Papa[20] or any of the others yet and instead of writing a long letter, if you would send this and my other letter to them, they would know something about what I am doing. Am glad they thought little Rebecca was so sweet. Ethel and I were over to the Consul's office yesterday. Found our way all alone. We were so proud. We must not be out after five o'clock by ourselves.

Do not know just how long we will be here, ten days or two weeks. Write me often.

Love to you all, Nancy[21]

The hospitable John Edward Jones also arranged an overnight trip to Monte Carlo for his guests leaving on June 14 about the ferry *France*. John Young and Mr. Laugieri, both dressed in jaunty suits and straw hats, and carrying canes, accompanied the new arrivals around Monaco's capital. Nancy particularly enjoyed the flower gardens and her introduction to the world famous Casino, the international society's playground, even though she quickly lost a good deal of money at the gaming tables. She also enjoyed the special attention she received from the charming Consul General Jones. He had sent her off to Monte Carlo with a bouquet of four orchids and a box of candy. Though Nancy had no desire to become the new Mrs. Jones, she was thrilled by his attentions and also by the fact that Ethel did not get as much as she did. Nancy wore Jones's flowers on her jacket while she toured Monte Carlo. A small pang of guilt made her give the box of candy to Ethel. After a delightful motorcar ride to Nice, the company spent the night there in a beautiful hotel. The next morning they returned to Monte Carlo in time to catch the ferryboat back to Genoa. This side adventure cost a lot of money, but Nancy enjoyed every expensive moment of it. She promised herself to watch her pennies when they got to Venice.

Nancy Johnson and Ethel
Norris aboard the ferry *France*
going from Genoa to Monte
Carlo, Monaco. Caption on
the back of the photograph in
Nancy's handwriting: "Notice
my orchids given me by
the Consul-General" (John
Edward Jones). June 14, 1914

On the ferry *France* going from Genoa to Monte Carlo, Monaco (L to R): Ethel,
Mr. Laugieri (U.S. consulate's Italian courier), Nancy, and John Barclay Young
(U.S. vice-consul in Genoa). June 14, 1914

On the ferry *France:* Ethel, Mr. Laugieri, John Barclay Young, and Dr. B. Harvey Carroll. June 14, 1914

Once back in Genoa, Nancy, Ethel, and the Carrolls made ready to travel on to Venice by way of Milan. At this point, Nancy was offered the opportunity to travel to Rome to fulfill her mother's dearest wish, but Nancy decided to forgo an audience with Pope Pius X. Since the summer weather had turned hot, she had no desire to dress up in heavy black clothes—the traditional garb for an audience with the supreme pontiff of the Catholic Church. Besides, she did not want to inconvenience the non-Catholic Carrolls, who were anxious to reach Venice. More to the point, the trip to Rome would incur additional costs.

Decades later, Nancy shrugged off her decision. "How was I to know that the pope was going to become a saint?"[22]

On Monday morning, June 22, Nancy, Ethel, and the Carrolls finally boarded the train for Venice, again accompanied by Vice Consul Young as their guide. They changed trains in Milan, where they paused in their journey and spent an enjoyable overnight visit. Young escorted Nancy and Ethel on a tour of the beautiful cathedral and, of more interest to the young women, the Galleria, one of the largest shopping arcades in Europe.

In Monte Carlo, Monaco (L to R): John Young, Nancy, Ethel, Mr. Laugieri, and Daisy Carroll. June 14, 1914

Identified on the back of the photograph in Nancy's handwriting: "Mr. Young and Nancy, 'The Galleria' in Milan." June 22, 1914

On the train from Milan to Venice. June 23—

My dear Father—

To try to describe all that we see—every minute of the time—even the scenery that we are passing now is too far beyond me. We left Milan at six o'clock so as to reach Venice by moonlight. We are due there at eleven.

We are now just passing Lake Gorda [*sic*],[23] that along with Como being the most beautiful in the world. From Genoa, we went Sunday morning [June 14] by boat to Monte Carlo. We have had rather an expensive trip, which we really could not well afford, but far more important we could not afford to be so near and miss it. The Consul General is responsible, as he almost made us take it, and we cannot thank him enough. He sent his Vice-Consul, a young fellow, along with us. He is Mr. Young[24]—a cousin of the Howard girls in Washington. I am ashamed to tell you that at Monte Carlo I lost twenty francs—four dollars.[25] One is not allowed to play less than five franc [*sic*] at a time and the first time Mr. Young won and if I had only played with him, and then afterwards every time I would play with him he would lose and win when I was out. But I soon saw that it was a losing game. He did well when he quit even. I saw one man win almost a thousand dollars[26] at one swoop. This is not the season for Monte Carlo— and consequently not the interesting crowds that are there in the winter. Monte Carlo is in the principality of Monaco, about fifteen square miles. The prince[27] owns the bank. His subjects pay no taxes and are not allowed to play. It is built right on the Mediterranean and in the most ideal spot one can conceive. That night we took the train from Monte Carlo to Nice —and went to a lovely hotel Du Rhin. My [*sic*] presenting Dr. Jones' card we got very good rates. From Nice the next day we went back to Monte Carlo by motor—to get a view of the Italian Riviera and see the famous ride—Le Grande Cornich, right along the cliffs of the Alps, bordering the sea. The road was as smooth as a boulevard, but up, up the mountain side and off in the distance but plainly visible the snow-covered tops of the higher peaks. The evenings are the loveliest times. The twilight lingers so long, and the whole earth has those various colors and tints that could not be seen any place but Italy.

I will be glad to get to Venice and settle down, there we will be at a very nice pension on the Grand canal [*sic*] at about $1.50 a day.[28] Just as we guessed Dr. Carroll will be a little hard up for cash, but he is absolutely honest to the smallest detail. He had to borrow some from the Consul general [*sic*]. Mrs. Carroll is lovely, plain and sweet and every one likes her. We have surely been shown curtesies [*sic*] and attention by being with the

Carrolls that we could not otherwise have gotten—and they are most thoughtful and kind to Ethel and me.

At Milan Ethel and I did not like the hotel. We wanted to save expenses and as we were there only one night it really did not matter, but I do like to stop at nice hotels. It was a very quiet nice family hotel, Mr. Young said.

I cannot begin to tell you how I appreciate the advantages you are giving me. This trip is something that can never be taken from me.[29] So far it has been much more expensive than I thought, travelling here is not cheap, but after we get to Venice, it will be different. We are expecting our gondola to meet us to-night. I will let you know later when I will need money— probably about the first of August.

We are coming now to some city, I think Verona.

I wrote to Clemence's Mother.[30] If you are going to be perfectly willing I think I would like to stay in Europe until April [1915]. To leave the first of December would be too soon, and I must wait then until the ocean gets calmer. Mother has been very good about writing. Her letter was forwarded to me from Venice. Do have her write often, and I will write at least once a week. From now on there will not be so much to tell. Write me all about your run for Congress, etc. Mrs. Ayres surely was nice in her writings to me.[31] I hope that you and Mother will sometime know what a trip to Europe is.

With all my very best love to Anita and you all—Nancy[32]

Around 11 P.M., the train rolled across the long causeway to the city that appeared to float on the moonlit waters of the lagoon—Venice! "The traveler emerging for the first time upon the terrace of the railway station seems to have a Canaletto before him," observed Henry James.[33] By midnight, Nancy and Ethel were ensconced in their new home for their stay in Venice—Pensione Gregory. Then the Carrolls left the two young women and went on to the American consulate at Number 1408 on the Fondamenta della Zattere, a three-story house overlooking the wide Giudecca Canal. Meanwhile Nancy and Ethel surveyed their new surroundings with growing dismay. Their room looked like it would crumble away at any moment. Nancy went to bed feeling not only homesick but also extremely sorry for herself. However, the following morning the newcomers soon learned that dilapidation was an art form in Venice. Moreover, their *pensione* was considered one of the best places for Americans to stay in Venice, and the meals were delicious.

Within a few days, Nancy and Ethel were enchanted by Venice, particularly the gondolas. On Friday evening, June 26, the Carrolls treated their guests to an evening ride down the Grand Canal in the consulate's gondola. Nancy and Ethel loved the nightly concert provided by the gondoliers near the Ducal Palace. To add to the magic of the night, a silver crescent moon hung in the blue-black velvet sky above the water. This experience was everything Nancy had dreamed Venice would be.

The following afternoon, Nancy wrote long letters home to her mother and her grandfather. Again, she dodged her family's plan for her to visit the Dutch cousins early in her trip. Now that she had fallen under Venice's spell, Nancy had no intention of cutting short her time there. Also, she realized that once she arrived in Holland, she would lose a portion of her newfound freedom. Knowing that her parents had received letters from the cousins, Nancy cited her mounting expenses as the main reason for postponing her trip to the Netherlands. Her ultimate goal was to live in Paris during the coming winter, so she spent a large portion of her letters writing lengthy explanations. In the letter to Papa, she acted as if she planned to remain single all her life. She did not betray the fact that Lieutenant Roscoe Crawford was still very much on her mind. It is probable that she also sent Roscoe long letters of her adventures, but if so, they have disappeared.

Venice

My dear Papa

I had two lovely letters, one from Clemence and one from Hubert[34] waiting for me here at Venice. Clemence will be married the twenty-seventh of August and wants me to come up for the wedding and then go to France or Switzerland and come back to them later and sail from there in April. They urge me to stay with them just as long as possible. But Clemence suggested that if only one trip to Holland could be made it would be better to ["make" crossed out] visit Holland last because Hubert has to serve in the army until the twentieth of September and Clemence will be away on her honey moon trip. While I would love to be there for the wedding still I believe it would be better to stay in Italy until August or September and then if Mrs. Ives comes to Switzerland to stay a month with her then try to find some place, possibly a school in France, or rather Paris for November and December, and then to Holland and stay until April. I will write to Clemence immediately, but will wait until I hear from home[35] before making any definite arrangements. Hubert said he had written to Father asking him to let me make two trips to Holland and stay until April, but it seems that could be too expensive. And it would be much nicer to be in Holland while Hubert and Clemence are there and after all the excitement of the wedding is over. Clemence described her new home to me. It sounds most attractive. Will enclose the picture she sent me one of their home and the other of her future husband.

From Genoa we went to Monte-Carlo and that was a most expensive luxury. I lost twenty francs. The Consul General at Genoa sent his Vice Consul, a very nice going fellow, to be our guide at Monte Carlo and Nice and Milan. I was playing with him but he would lose every time with me, and win when I was not playing. The Consul General was so nice to us. I went out with him one afternoon and he bought me the loveliest bunch of orchids. Four immense ones on one stem, and he also bought a large box of candy which I took back to Ethel Norris. He could not have been nicer, and if I were only a young heiress I would land him—three children and all. But it is settled that I am to be an old maid. It is really much nicer to be satisfied with that lot. But back to other things more important. Congressman Sharpe [sic], whose wife's brother married Cousin Edna Cerelter, has been made Ambassador to France and I know Mrs. Sharpe [sic],[36] it could be wonderfully nice for me to be in Paris a while this winter. Nice and Milan I think are charming, but Venice is so distinctive that all its beauty and quaintness make my descriptive powers dumb. We arrived at about eleven o'clock at night, and we were met by the Vice Consul[37] in the gondola belonging to the Consulate. The gondolier was wearing white with a wide red sash and red band on his arm with the large brass emblem of the U.S. Our gondola is quite one of the handsomest ones. I will take some pictures and send you. The only trouble is that the gondolier is kept so busy at the office that we get very little use of him. Last night we had the most beautiful time! We went up to the lagoon on the Grand Canal and heard the singing. The musicians were in a gondola all decorated with lanterns and our gondola along with numbers of others held to it, and drifted. Some of the voices were very good. After each piece a man went from one gondola to the other collecting pennies. There was a small crescent moon and my picture of Venice has even done it full credit. We are staying at a very nice pensione on the Grand Canal, Pensione Gregory. I like it now, but my first impression was very disappointing and I feared I would not like it much. The houses all seemed so old and decayed. Some of them lean and look as though they would fall any time. St. Mark's Square is quite the most beautiful I have seen.

Please send this letter out to Rebecca and let it be for all of you. It is so hard to write so many letters and tell the same things. My next one will be to her. I hope I am going to like to stay here in Venice. It is sometimes hard

Nancy and Ethel
sightseeing in Milan,
June 22, 1914

to be entirely congenial when living so intimately with persons.[38] Rebecca
and Hendy must write and tell me all about the children. Write me how
mamma[39] is. I wrote Aunt Ella[40] from Genoa. Guess she has gotten it. My
love to her and Dan.

Very best to all of you—Nancy
June 27/14
Care Dr. Carroll
American Consulate

[Written in William Kouwenbergh's hand] Rebecca, your mother asked
that all of Nancy's letters be saved for future reference; please take care of
this one. How are you all? With love—Papa[41]

Like most young people on their first trip abroad, Nancy censored her
letters to the various members of her family. She wrote essentially the same

Daisy Carroll, Ethel, and Nancy in the American consulate's gondola, Venice, July 1914

information to her mother as she had to her grandfather, but she "neglected" to mention several things: that she had gambled away twenty francs in Monte Carlo's Casino; that two members of their party in Monte Carlo and overnight in Nice were young, handsome bachelors; and the fact that she planned to spend the winter in Paris instead of returning to the States or going to Holland. In her letters, Nancy skillfully maneuvered her mother and grandfather into believing that the idea for extending her sojourn in Europe to a year had originated with her Dutch cousins instead of herself. Again, Nancy was quite firm in her decision not to go to Rome. In her letters to her father, she was more open about her plans. She knew he would forgive her almost anything short of murder or dishonor.

Venice

My dear Mother

I wrote to Father on the train coming to Venice and I am glad I did, as after seeing Venice it will be impossible to go back and tell about any other place. My first impression was all that I had anticipated. We got in about eleven o'clock, after travelling over a bridge about two miles long built through the water connecting Venice to the main land. We were met by the

Vice Consul in the gondola belonging to the Consulate. It is a very hand-some one, about twenty-five feet in length, cushioned seats and finished up beautifully, but the cutest part is the old gondolier, wearing a white suit, with flowing red sash and band on his arm with a large brass emblem of the U.S. The pity is that most of the gondoliers do not dress attractively and the gondolas are being replaced with launches, which takes away much of the picturesqueness (I can't spell it) of the place. Upon arriving at our pensione—boarding house—I had a shock, and thought I would not like it. The houses are all very old and decayed, looking as though they were ready to fall into the water any minute, and some of the handsome old palaces are leaning worse than the Tower of Pisa. They say that they will stand for centuries more. Here at the Pensione Gregory we must go up three flights of stairs as the part below is occupied by some one else, and we have a separate side entrance. We have not gotten our regular rooms yet, and that first night when Dr. and Mrs. Carroll left us way off in the back of the house alone in a large bare room—I gave up and felt as though I had not a friend in the world. The next morning at breakfast was not much better as all these old boarding house cats began to appear, most of them Americans. But when I saw the meals we were going to have and got used to all the houses and palaces looking the same dilapidated condition, I became more cheerful. I suppose it is Venice.[42] It is almost the best in Venice. It is quite well known and the Vice Consul said that Roosevelt's son and daughter, I suppose Ethel, stayed here.

We do not know the people yet, but they seem very nice and elegant. Ethel and Mrs. Carroll are much more congenial than I am. Do not tell Mrs. Norris this, but I do not mind that part of it, if I can manage to get along pleasantly with them. Ethel has been very nice and tries to be, but sometimes her naturally selfish <u>disposition</u> shows a little.[43] But I do not mind her, she can't help it—and so far we have gotten along beautifully. Dr. and Mrs. Carroll both like me, especially Dr. Carroll.

I wrote to Clemence's Mother from Genoa and when I got here I had two very long letters, one from Clemence and one from Hubert, who was writing for his Mother. They were most cordial and urged me to come and stay as long as I could. I will enclose their letters if I can. The pictures Clemence sent I forwarded to Papa. Have just written to him. I have just tried and their letters are so thick I guess I cannot send them. Hubert said he had written to Father, and I guess he told him practically the same thing. That they would love for me to come to the wedding & then if I wanted to make a visit to France go there and then back to ["Italy" scratched out]

Holland and sail from there in April. But if only one visit to Holland could be made, it would be better to come later, so I could stay in Europe longer and then Clemence & Hubert would both be at home. Hubert serves in the army until the 20th of Sept. Clemence will live in the Hague and has described her new home which sounds most attractive. She wants me to visit her some. What I would like you to do is this—Find out right away for me if Mrs. Ives is coming to Switzerland. Then go from here to Switzerland and stay the last of August & Sept. with her then to France and stay until about January the first, then go to Holland & stay until April. That is the sensible plan, as my trip has already been more expensive than I thought. I must stay in one place long enough now to save up some. Our trip to Nice and Milan was very expensive and our trunks have cost so much. By the way my trunk has not gotten here yet. The others just came this morning, sent on from Genoa when we landed, and mine is not with them. Am sure though it will be all right. It takes so long here. My money is beginning to get low. If you will send me some to get here the first part of August. Will have plenty until then. Mrs. Norris sends Ethel a check. You can find out how she sent it. On some bank, I think.[44]

I think it better to give up the idea of going to Rome. I really do not care so much and as it is quite some distance would be very expensive, and I have seen so much of Italy would prefer going some where else. Besides I do not know of any to go with. In France I would like to stay at some school. There are no convents there. But that seems to be the cheapest and nicest thing. Being alone it is about all I could do. I can't imagine any thing being nicer that to be there with the Sharps as Ambassador.[45] Especially would the winter months be nice. I am very ambitious for that. And will leave Rome to see some other time, on my numerous other trips to Europe. Do see the Ives and let me hear. And try to learn from them some place in France where I could stay and I will write and get prices. It is so hard to wait so long to hear from you. By now of course you have gotten my first letter but that was written so long ago I have almost forgotten what I wrote. Do not fail to write often. Remember I am pretty far off and alone.[46]

The Consul general [sic] at Genoa has been so lovely. He sends us the Washington Stars[47] and while we were there could not do enough. He was at one time a reporter on the Star, and quite a friend of the Noyes.[48] Mr. Young, his Vice Consul is a cousin of the Howards, so as not mention him much before Margaret McChord. He took us out several times to the theatre and one afternoon I went out with him and he bought me the loveliest orchids, four perfectly immense ones on one stem, and also a box of candy to take home to Ethel. He says if every one doesn't treat me just right tell him and he will give them the deuce. The Carrolls stand very much in awe of him as he is Dr. Carroll's direct boss. I did not let Ethel know that I believe he liked me a little better, but tried to impress upon her that he didn't, which perhaps he didn't. He really did everything for us.

It is now nearly luncheon time.

Lots and lots of love—Nancy

June 27/14
[In Annie Johnson's hand] Save all letters.[49]

While the Carrolls settled into their new duties in Venice, Nancy and Ethel finished their unpacking and wrote long letters home. The next morning, June 28, they took their first opportunity to go out on their own and see the famous sights of this most unique city in the world, where the streets were "paved with ripples."[50] After Nancy attended Sunday Mass, she and Ethel toured the doge's pink palace and walked around the gilded basilica of Saint Mark's Cathedral. It looked more like a palace out of *The Arabian Nights* than Saint Joseph's Proto-Cathedral back home in Bardstown, Nancy thought. The day was bright and sunny, and the great square of Saint Mark's was filled with holidaymakers. It was hard to believe that she had already been on her Grand Tour for a whole month and was just now starting on Venice. Nancy excitedly looked forward to the weeks ahead.

"Some damn foolish thing in the Balkans"[51] would spark the next major war, predicted Bismarck, Germany's great chancellor.[52] On June 28, 1914, his prophetic words came true.

Archduke Franz Ferdinand, nephew of the Austrian emperor and heir to the throne, was a sour, embittered man of fifty-one years. The only person in the world who truly loved him was Sophie, his morganatic wife, whom Franz had married over his royal uncle's strenuous objections. In court circles, she was known only as the Duchess of Hohenberg. Yet as the passing years proved, their marriage was one of the few royal matches that was cemented by a mutual, abiding love. When the archduke was invited to visit the city of Sarajevo in Bosnia, he seized upon this rare opportunity to give Sophie the full royal honors she so richly deserved.

The morning of June 28 dawned clear and bright all over southern Europe. While Nancy crossed the Ponte dell'Accademia bridge over the Grand Canal to mail her letter to her mother at Venice's main post office, 319 miles away seven of the most unlikely assassins gathered in the streets of Sarajevo to change the course of modern history.

June 28 was not only Archduke Ferdinand and his wife's fourteenth wedding anniversary, but it was also the feast day of Saint Vitas, as well as the local anniversary of the battle of Kosovo, a medieval victory over the hated Turks. Sarajevo was bedecked with colorful flags, and the populace standing along the archduke's parade route were in a holiday mood.

Scattered among the happy crowd, the young terrorists waited for their prey. Calling themselves the Black Hand, these fanatics were motivated by a confused sense of Serbian nationalism. Despite their vague ideology, their purpose was deadly. They were armed with an assortment of homemade bombs and pistols, as well as cyanide capsules to be swallowed in case of capture.

As the royal procession motored down the street on its way to the town hall, the first would-be assassin lost his nerve and melted back into the crowd. Farther down the route, the second young man, Nedjelko Cabrinovic, threw a grenade at the royal car; however, the driver took evasive action and speeded up. The bomb bounced off the back of the archduke's car and rolled onto the street, where it detonated under the second car in the procession, injuring several members of the archduke's court as well as several spectators on the sidewalk. Cabrinovic swallowed his poison pill, and then jumped off a nearby bridge into the river. Neither attempt killed him, but the crowd, who hauled him out of the water, almost did before the police could rescue him.

Though the archduke and Sophie were shaken by this attempt on their lives, they continued on to the town hall. Unbeknownst to them, their convertible passed three more members of the Black Hand, who did nothing but stare at the royals. Once at the town hall, the archduke lost his temper at the mayor in the midst of the poor man's speech of welcome.

"Herr Burgermeister, it is perfectly outrageous! We have come to Sarajevo on a visit and we have had a bomb thrown at us!" The archduke then paused during his tirade, swallowed the rest of his ire, and said, "Now you may go on with your speech."[53]

After the formalities at the town hall concluded, the archduke told his driver to make a side trip to the hospital where the injured members of his party had been taken. En route, the chauffeur missed the turn toward the hospital. He stopped the car, backed it up, and then shifted his gears to complete the turn-around. Lurking in a doorway less than five feet away was eighteen-year-old Gavrilo Princip,[54] the sixth member of the Black Hand. No one looked in his direction as he pulled his pistol from inside his jacket.

Princip darted forward and fired two rounds at the royal couple at point blank range. Startled by the gunfire, the chauffeur let go of the clutch, and the car jerked forward. The first shot struck Sophie in the abdomen, while the second shot hit the archduke in the neck. The duchess lost consciousness immediately. Slowly she fell across her husband's knees. A few seconds later, the archduke slumped in his seat, his jugular vein spouting blood. The chauffeur slammed the car into gear and drove to the royal palace. The archduke and his wife were pronounced dead on arrival. Since both Princip and his co-conspirator, Cabrinovic, were Bosnian-Serbs, it was immediately assumed that they were the spearheads of a political plot organized by Serbian nationalists for unification.[55]

International reaction and shock were almost immediate as the wireless flashed the news of the assassination around Europe and across the Atlantic. However, only a few men gifted with sharp political insight grasped the possible significance of the killings. Future U.S. president Herbert Hoover,[56] then a young mining engineer on a business trip to London, later wrote in his memoirs: "On June 28th, 1914, when news came of the assassination of the Archduke at Sarajevo, the world took it as just another one of those habitual Balkan lapses into barbarism—and we went about our accustomed business with little more thought than that."[57]

In Paris, Nicholas Butler heard the shouting of the newsboys from his hotel window. Though shocked by the news, the president of Columbia University did not think that the double murder would result in a worldwide conflict. "It did not occur to any of us as at all possible," he later wrote.[58] The following day, June 29, the Butlers left Paris and began their leisurely motor trip through the beautiful French countryside.

No doubt, B. Harvey Carroll, the American consul in Venice, learned the news within the first twenty-four hours. Shocking though it was, the double killings of the heir to the Austro-Hungarian throne and his wife did not seem to disturb his sense of security, nor did it frighten his wife and their young guests. Being infatuated with royal families, Nancy probably read the account of the murders in whatever English newspaper she could find, but the assassination was more fodder for speculation over a cup of delicious coffee than a wake-up call to world chaos. Nancy and Ethel continued to fill their days with their leisurely pursuit of sightseeing, shopping, and Italian ice cream.

Nancy adored Saint Mark's Square, and she returned to it often with Ethel. Napoleon once described this huge plaza as "the drawing room of Europe." Nancy delighted in the antics of the hundreds of pigeons that begged for corn, the music that someone was always playing in the square, and the twilight promenade of the locals and visitors alike when everyone showed off their finery. Most of all she loved to sit at one of the many little round café tables that hugged the sides of the huge square and drink coffee or eat a bowl of Italy's incomparable gelato. One of Nancy's favorite cafés was Caffe Florian, located near the basilica.

Even into the twenty-first century, Caffe Florian is still one of the most famous of the coffee shops in the Piazza San Marco. It was established in 1720, making it not only the oldest coffeehouse in Venice but also in Italy. It is reputed that Caffe Florian was the place where Europeans first tasted the caffeinated Turkish drink, coffee. It has long been a meeting place for artists and writers. Among Caffe Florian's many famous patrons were Mark Twain, Johann Goethe, Marcel Proust, Thomas Mann, and Ernest Hemingway. Caffe Florian is also one of the most expensive coffeehouses in Venice, but it is considered a "must see" for all visitors to the city.[59]

Perhaps the most amazing sight that Nancy saw during one of her visits to Caffe Florian was a troupe of American cowboys and Indians—the latter dressed in full feathers, beads, and buckskins—who sat around several tables nearby, smoking cigarettes and drinking coffee. Young Venetian boys, usually jaded by the thousands of foreign visitors, stared with open astonishment at the extraordinary costumes. The men were members of an American Wild West show that had come to perform in Venice. Seated at her table, Nancy surreptitiously sighted the odd group in her camera viewfinder and snapped the most interesting photo on her roll of film. Consul General Jones had not exaggerated when he had told her that everyone in the world came to Saint Mark's Square sooner or later.

While Nancy and Ethel strolled around Venice, practiced their Italian on unsuspecting natives, and savored more gelato, events in eastern Europe were leading to actions that would alter everyone's vacation plans within the next month—and for years to come. By July 1, the loose webs of Europe's multilayered alliances began to tighten in the wake of the capture of the archduke's killers. Seizing upon the confessions of the two idealistic young men as a pretext for punitive action against Serbia, Austria-Hungary decided to annex the troublesome little country in order to keep it under tighter control. Germany's Kaiser Wilhelm grasped at this opportunity to demonstrate Germany's growing power. He blithely gave his complete assurances to Austria that it could count on Germany's support in case Austria's conflict with Serbia would bring Russia, Serbia's ally, into the fray. Having made this impetuous, but binding, promise, Wilhelm then departed for the fjords of Norway for a three-week pleasure cruise aboard his yacht, the *Hohenzollern*. In his wake, the kaiser left an escalating chain of events that headed Germany on a course of eventful ruin with the speed of a runaway train.

To complicate matters for all concerned, during the first week of July Europe was blanketed by a sirocco, an energy-draining heat wave blown north

American cowboys and Indians from a traveling Wild West show, photographed by Nancy at Caffe Florian in Saint Mark's Square, Venice, late July 1914

Nancy's caption on the back of this photograph identifies the gentleman as "Mr. Laugieri." Saint Mark's Square, Venice, late July 1914

from the hot sands of Africa's Sahara Desert. The weather turned everyone nervous and cranky. Even Nancy and Ethel, who were used to Washington's torrid summers, retreated to the cool, darkened rooms of their *pensione* and waited for the relief that their landlady assured them would come soon.

While Nancy fanned herself and ate more ice cream, Annie Johnson fretted her way through Washington's usual summertime languor. In early July, she finally received Nancy's letter of June 27 and was crushed by the news that her daughter had bypassed the opportunity to meet the pope in Rome. On July 5, Annie began a letter that would take her the better part of a week to complete.

1620 S Street [Washington, D.C.]

My dear Nancy,

It is hot as can be! Sam is here to take dictation; we have just finished our Sunday dinner [July 5] which was unusually good to me as we had fried chicken of our own killing.

I hardly know how to begin as I seem to have so much I want to say. I have been rather remiss about writing you recently. I believe it has been about ten days, but I wanted to get some addresses and other information for you, which delayed me. I will also enclose a draft for you for $100.00 of our money. Mrs. Ansberry[60] advised your father to send it this way.

Yesterday I tried to telephone Berry & Whitmore[61] for advice about a present for Clemence but could get no one. I will talk to them and see if it would be feasible to send something from here, or whether you should buy it there.

I had a sewing woman, a negro, five days; and she is a treasure. She made me a lovely white crepe with a [*sic*] small lavender flowers (from Louisville) and a blue silk with tiny white dots. They are stylish as can be. The woman is the one Mrs. Beall[62] always has. I telephoned Mrs. Norris to come over yesterday and she spent the day. She is going to have the seamstress make her a silk. She made the McChords lovely things, and went from me to Mrs. Folk.

I tried to get Ramona's address yesterday but failed. Will telephone again before sending this. Mrs. Ives promised to give me Paris addresses. She does not know what she is going to do. Joe failed on his physical examination (eyes). Your father is trying to get another for him. Thinks he will be able to do so through Secretary Daniels,[63] but he is out of town just now. Did I tell you Mrs. D. wrote to Mrs. Ives she would like for Margaret[64] to join you? It is so hard to try to make plans at this distance. Your ideas seem all right but we would be sorry for you to miss Rome.

The Sharps all took dinner with us and want to see you in Paris. Mrs. Sharp said she wanted us <u>all</u> to visit her when she is settled. She looks lovely; but is not well, and her Dr. will not allow her to go on until December. Mr. Sharp and the oldest boy will go in Aug. Mrs. S. said she hoped you would not go until she is there, but if you did you must look up Mr. S. He will board until she arrives. (he will return for her.) They have engaged their predecessor's[65] social secretary & will rent the same house. ($15,000) Is'ent [sic] it just fine?

I stopped here to run over to Mrs. Ives.' As I was saying on her paper you might try this place Mlle. Cheverean, for a while; have Mlle. Lessier who lives there teach you french [sic] & chaperone you when necessary. Then when you want to do some society, if you think it necessary you might spend that time at the first place, which is kept by the Sisters, &, as I understand it, is quite exclusive. Their place in Belgium would be nice, close to Paris, but I don't know how cheap. But I am sure where Mrs. Ives was would suit you. Admiral Cowles is Roosevelt's brother-in-law I think. I will get Ramona's address to-morrow; am anxious to get your money off. Let me know what you decide to do. Mrs. N. seems very anxious for Miss Ethel to go to Switzerland and France with you. If you think it would be pleasant and it would be better of course to have her with you. It is so late & your father is hurrying me to bed.

Now do be careful, & do not travel alone. My love for you all. Tell Dr. & Mrs. Carroll we appreciate so much what they are doing for you. Goodnight!

July 11th. Devotedly, Mother[66]

By mid-July, the sirocco had not yet abated. The plazas of Venice emptied during midday as tourists and natives alike sought relief in the darkened rooms of their houses and hotels. Also it was healthier to stay indoors as Venice's "fever season" was about to begin. The only time it was comfortable to come out was after dark. On July 13, the Carrolls entertained Nancy and Ethel as well as some other guests with dinner and the nightly gondoliers' concert on the Grand Canal. Ethel had been suffering from an earache, but Nancy talked her into going out anyway. At the end of the pleasant evening, Vice Consul Leon di Sauvanne escorted the young women back to their *pensione,* which was located off on a side street. Along the way, some drunken men accosted the party. Sauvanne called to the women and told them to cross the canal at the nearby bridge and go around down another street. The men began to chase after the women at a dead run. Nancy and Ethel fled across the bridge with their hearts in their throats. Meanwhile Sauvanne placed himself at the foot of the bridge, took off his hat, unbuttoned his coat, and stared down at the drunks. Fortunately the ruffians were sober enough to recognize their danger, and they backed off. Nancy and Ethel returned to their lodgings in a state of near hysteria.

The next morning, July 14, Ethel's earache was worse, perhaps inflamed by the damp night air or by her fright of the previous evening. Nancy had already taken her to a local doctor, recommended by their landlady, but he did not seem to do much for Ethel except to charge an outrageous fee for his services. Ethel retired to her bed while Nancy used this unexpected free time to continue working on her correspondence. She wrote a long-overdue letter to her older sister in which she could be more candid about her escapades in Italy. Nancy related the story of the disturbing incident, one that she knew would frighten both her parents if they learned of it. She did not want to be ordered home just yet. On the other hand, now that the danger had passed, Nancy relished spinning her tale of dark streets and lurking ruffians just to show her big sister all the "fun" and excitement she was missing in Kentucky.

Venice

My Dear Rebecca,

Have been wanting to write you, but having so many letters to write it is hard to get around. Especially hard when each one costs a nickel. Over here one learns the value of pennies.

I guess you were really surprised to hear that I was coming, but you could not have been more so than I. Mother said she was sending my letters so it will not be necessary to tell you all that I have done. We have now found a lovely place, very inexpensive and nice, so I feel that I am settled for a little while at least. I am most anxious to stay in Europe until April. Have just written Maryann [sic] Druin[67] to learn if they are coming to Switzerland. Venice has been very cool and comfortable with the exception of a few days. But those few days have been awfully warm. There is a very hot wind that comes from the Sahara Desert, that sweeps over all Southern Italy, and we are feeling that same now. They call it the Cirocca [sic]. So if I could get into the mountains of Switzerland, it would be much more comfortable, and I could gradually work myself North to Holland. I should be afraid to travel alone here.

Last night I was scared to death. We were coming home with Mr. De Sauvanne [sic], the Vice Consul here, when he saw some drunken men coming, so he called us back to cross over a little bridge & go another way to avoid them. They saw us, and one started in a run after us. Ethel & I hurried ahead, and Mr. De Sauvanne waited for him. When he saw Mr. De Sauvanne ready to fight he stopped short & we came home without further trouble. Those Italians!

Ethel wants me to go down town with her now. Poor thing, she is having trouble with her ear, and is so distressed. We went to the doctor yesterday and he charged her two dollars[68] and did no good at all. Supposed to have washed it out, but it is worse this morning.

Do write me and tell me about the children. I have little Rebecca's picture with me, sitting up very prominently on the bureau. Ethel and I talk about her all the time. Ethel thinks she is the cutest thing. Mother wrote me that she won the whole train over on the way home. Hope Ben Johnson[69] has been well. Give my love to Dan and all the Talbotts.[70] Has William married and in Sheridan or home?

It takes so long to get a letter over here. I sometimes feel as though I were cut off from every body.

Love from Nancy

July 14/14[71]

The two women's frightening experience deeply concerned Carroll. Obviously it was not safe to let Nancy and Ethel wander about those small side streets after dark, and Vice Consul Sauvanne could not always be their escort. Carroll decided that the best thing for all concerned would be to move Nancy and Ethel into the consulate, where they would be more protected and where he would be able to know what plans they had for each day. He had no desire to have to explain to the hot-tempered Ben Johnson why his beloved daughter Nancy had been robbed—or worse. He sent a message to the *pensione* that the young women should pack their bags at once. Nancy was not only relieved but also delighted. The move to the consulate also seemed to shake the earache out of Ethel.

Bright and early on July 15, Nancy and Ethel said their last good-byes to their fellow guests at Pensione Gregory and took the consulate's gondola to 1408 Zattere, located on the wide Giudecca Canal. They had barely settled in their new quarters when a young American woman, who had been on her honeymoon in Venice, arrived on the consulate's doorstep in great distress. Her new husband had just died of a sudden fever, probably typhoid, in their honeymoon suite. Now the new widow was alone in Venice and did not know what to do.

With her ingrained horror of death, Nancy wanted to retreat from the scene. Ethel, on the other hand, forgot her earache and rose to the occasion.

With her natural empathy and warmth, she calmed and comforted the bereaved young woman, while B. Harvey Carroll began the necessary arrangements for transporting the body and the widow back to the United States. With both B. Harvey Carroll and Ethel busy with the young widow, Daisy Carroll was left with the task of going to their hotel and packing up the couple's belongings. She immediately enlisted the reluctant Nancy to help her. For the first time since Nancy had arrived in Europe, she finally understood that a consul's job was not all parties and concerts. Living at the consulate might provide more security, better accommodations, and good meals, but it had a price.

With the sirocco still hovering over Venice, and now with the first signs that the annual fever had arrived, Nancy became anxious to leave for the cooler, healthier climes of Switzerland. Though she loved Venice, she thought it was high time to move on before something else unpleasant happened.

On July 16, Nancy wrote to her father. By now she desperately needed more money, not knowing that her mother had already mailed a bank draft to her on July 11. Nancy had probably written an earlier letter concerning the American bridal widow to one of her parents, but that letter has disappeared.

[Venice] July 16/14

My dear Father

It seemed so long before I got an answer to my letter, and as it is I have only had one short one. There is not so much that I can write now, we are not doing much. Venice has been too warm the last few days even for sightseeing. But where we are living now on the broad water front away from the narrow streets there is always some breeze and the nights are rather comfortable. The fleas are the worst bother & sometimes they almost can eat us up. But I am making up for all else by the amount I am eating. My appetite is enormous and I must have gained several pounds as my clothes are even getting tight in the belts.

A Dr. MacGlothlin, a teacher in the Baptist Seminary at Louisville and his wife & children, friends of the Carrolls, passed through Venice the other day on their way to Switzerland, and Ethel and I and possibly Mrs. Carroll want to leave here about the first of August and join them up in the mountains. Ethel & I are very anxious to get to Switzerland and think that a very good opportunity. Mother wrote me that Ramona was going & would like to have me join her but I have heard nothing from her and do not know her address so of course there is no way to reach her. If I hear that the Ives are coming, I shall arrange to join them. I am afraid it is not very healthy to stay in Venice during the hot month.

I wrote Mother that I would need money about the first of August so if you can send me a hundred dollars[72] as soon as you get this, if you have not already sent some, as I will especially need it very much then if we go to Switzerland. The last month I have done very well as I managed to get through July on about forty-five dollars.[73] At the end of the month I will have about twenty dollars[74] left, but that will not go far if we are travelling, although to get to the north of Switzerland from here will not cost more than ten dollars.[75] Then on to Paris is not much farther, and I must be there a while and then Holland is not so far. Get Mother to get the names of some schools in Paris from Mrs. Ives. I believe they would make an exception and let me board there. There are no convents in France, but must surely be some Catholic schools. In the northern part of Switzerland they speak French so I will begin studying there and with the rest of the time over here I could surely learn to speak it well. I do not believe it would take me long to learn some Italian. It is perfectly surprising how I have gotten to love all this old place, with all its dirt and some evil ordors [sic]. The exquisite beauty fully makes up for it all. Of course they [sic] can be no horses or carriages and every one walks mostly and this way I have learned to find my way around through the winding old streets. No two run straight or the same way, and are so narrow that in some of them a raised umbrella touches both sides of the stone walls. Of course though these open out into large courts. St. Mark's is wonderful. Am going to have a Kodak picture taken with the pigeons. When the cannon goes off at twelve o'clock they come into the square by the thousands to be fed and will light [sic] all around you, even on you. I believe they say that Napoleon brought them over. Venice is full of the the [sic] history of Napoleon. He captured it and destroyed or carried away much of it, part has been re-stored. In the evening the band plays in the centre of St. Mark's and it is no exaggeration to say that the square is filled with at least ten or fifteen thou-sand of persons. The square is an enclosure formed by St. Mark's Church, the Royal Palace & two other long buildings, the streets opening into it by little arched ways. Of course there is no traffic & people sit at little tables, eating ice cream & listen [sic] to the music. To stand on the Post office steps & view it, it can be compared only to some wonderful stage setting.

The poor little girl who lost her husband is now on her way home. The body will not be sent until the eighteenth as there are so many formalities to be gone through with, before they will accept it. It was the most pathetic and awful experience I have ever gone through with. We had to pack all his things as of course she could not bear the sight of them. He was only sick four days. She came and stayed here until things were ready as she could leave, and her grief was terrible. She clung to Ethel every minute. Ethel had to even sleep with her. The poor little thing doesn't speak anything but English, does not even know the Italian money & had to travel to France alone to take her steamer.

Do not know what I would do with out Ethel. She is lots [*sic*] of comfort to me and we are getting along beautifully.

Write me sometime every thing that is happening.

Loads of love, Nancy[76]

This is the last known letter that Nancy wrote from Europe, though it is obvious that she wrote at least one more just before she left Venice on July 31 in order to let her parents know where she was headed. Her last letter or letters may have been caught in the upheaval of the war and never delivered.

CHAPTER 6

The Last Weeks of the Gilded Age

The heat wave continued throughout Europe. Despite the temperature and the festering political situation, American visitors continued to disembark at Southampton, Hamburg, Le Havre, Genoa, and other bustling seaports throughout Europe. The summer tourist season had reached its peak month.

In addition to millionaires and college boys, more than thirty thousand American schoolteachers, most of them young women, had arrived in Europe by the third week in July. In swirls of skirts and bobbing hats, the excited ladies boarded trains and were shunted from one edifying city to the next, following their package tour schedule to the letter. They fanned themselves with their guidebooks and hid from the blistering sun under their umbrellas as they trotted through Rome's Coliseum, Paris's Notre Dame, Germany's fairytale castles, and London's Hyde Park. They were unaware of the war clouds gathering over their heads. In the whirlwind of their dream trips, they could barely remember where they had been yesterday.

In spite of the lingering heat, Nancy and Ethel enjoyed one of Venice's annual colorful pageants that took place on Sunday, July 19. The Feast of Il Redentore commemorated the city's divine deliverance from the Black Plague that had killed nearly a third of the population between 1575 and 1577. In thanksgiving for their rescue, Venice's Council of Ten built a votive church on the island of Giudecca, nearly opposite the canal from the American consulate. Each year, all Venice rejoiced with special masses at the Church of the Redeemer, prayers, and processions of lighted candles.

On Saturday, July 18, the night before the great feast day, a fleet of gondolas, decorated with flowers and colorful paper lanterns, sailed down the Grand Canal and out into the lagoon. The lantern lights looked like thousands of glowing fireflies dancing on the face of the water. Families crowded in the boats enjoyed traditional nighttime picnics accompanied by music that floated back over the lagoon to the ears of the foreigners who crowded on their balconies, enjoying the romantic sight. Midnight brought showers of fireworks from the Lido's beach, and most of the participants stayed out on the lagoon to watch the peach-colored dawn.[1]

No one in Venice suspected that the Feast of Il Redentore would be the last holiday of unabashed merrymaking for the next five years.

As if in answer to the prayers of the feast day, the smothering heat wave showed hopeful signs of abating on Monday, July 20. In farm fields, rye, wheat, and barley ripened; their golden heads bowed with the weight of the coming harvest. At this point in time, over 120,000 American tourists were scattered into every corner of twenty-six European countries.

Following their journey through southern France and northern Italy, Nicholas Butler; his wife, Kate; and daughter, Sarah, parked their automobile on the mainland and took a boat into Venice. After checking into the Grand Hotel on the Grand Canal, the affable university president and his family strolled over to Saint Mark's Square to enjoy the evening's promenade and serenade.

In Cortina, Frederick and Louise Vanderbilt continued their stay amid the tall pines and cool air of the Alpine resort. The Miramonti Hotel was a delightful stop. "Red-cheeked maids, clad in those picturesque peasant costumes with short skirts and beaded bodices, smiled from morning till night as they cared for our wants," Louise Vanderbilt recalled.[2]

The Wild West show actors who had caused such interest in the Piazza San Marco were now deep in Poland, where the American cowboys and Indians continued to dazzle their audiences with feats of skillful archery, knife throwing, target shooting, rope twirling, pageantry, and magnificent riding on their beautifully trained horses and cow ponies.

Back in Venice, Nancy and Ethel had finally received letters from home with the anticipated checks. Now that they had money in hand, it was time to make plans for the next stage of their Grand Tour. Despite Nancy's pleas to her mother for names of people whom they might know to be in Switzerland in August, none had been mentioned in her mother's letters. Nancy was anxious to leave Venice, so she decided to go through Switzerland and on to Paris a little earlier than planned. At least she knew of places where she could stay in Paris. For her part, Ethel decided to accompany Nancy and stay with her in France, at least for the month. Ethel's original plan had been to meet with her family's friends in September and stay with them in Switzerland. Pleased with their confusing travel rearrangements, the two women dragged out their steamer trunks and began to reorganize their belongings.

Nancy feeding the pigeons in Saint Mark's Square, Venice, late July 1914. This is the photograph she promised to send to her family back home.

They did take time to go on a final sightseeing tour of Venice, this time with Nancy's camera in hand. They were accompanied once again by the ever-charming Mr. Laugieri, who had arrived from Genoa to act as the women's courier on their journey through Switzerland to Paris. The young gallant was delighted to escort Nancy and Ethel.

Since Nancy had promised her parents that she would have her picture taken with Saint Mark's pigeons,[3] they visited the piazza and posed for photos as they fed the greedy birds with corn purchased in paper cones from the ever-present vendors. On the way back to the consulate at the end of the delightful afternoon, Mr. Laugieri presented Nancy with a large bouquet of pink roses. Nancy posed with her flowers on a bridge crossing the Rio di San Gervasio[4] for the final picture on her roll. If Mr. Laugieri also purchased flowers for Ethel, there is neither record nor photo of his gift to her.

Nancy in Venice. Caption on the back in her handwriting: "My roses Mr. Laugieri
gave me." Late July 1914

The next day, Nancy and Ethel immersed themselves in a tornado of packing their trunks, cases, boxes, and bags. Wanting to escape the heat and foul odors of the canals, Daisy Carroll decided to accompany them for part of the way until Nancy and Ethel were settled in Paris. Daisy Carroll looked forward to getting into the mountains, where it would be cooler. B. Harvey Carroll made arrangements for their railway tickets. Mr. Laugieri no doubt groaned silently when he saw the mountain of baggage that appeared to double in size by the hour.

Nancy and Ethel also did some last minute shopping—lace from the island of Burano, strings of colored glass beads from Murano for sisters and friends, and packets of postcards with views of the city. Nancy purchased an album book of sepia-tinted photographs of Venice for her parents. Stopping at the Martin & Michieli Fotomateriale shop at 1300 Calle dell' Ascensione near the post office, Nancy gave her exposed roll of film to the proprietor, who promised to develop it as soon as possible.[5]

Nancy also purchased a vanity set made of pale green Murano glass decorated with gold filigree. She realized it was a highly impractical, fragile thing to buy at this early stage of her travels, but she could not pass it up. Mother would love to have the two bottles and the matching lidded jar on her dresser. Nancy wrapped them in many layers of tissue paper.[6]

The young women could hardly wait for Friday, July 31—the date of their departure. While Nancy had enjoyed her stay in Venice, it was definitely time to move on. In another month she would finally be settled in Paris!

On July 23, 1914, Austria-Hungary threw down the gauntlet on the European stage. The government sent an ultimatum to Serbia in retaliation for the assassination of Franz Ferdinand and his wife. The ultimatum was deliberately harsh, basically ordering Serbia to grovel in the dust. The Austrian government hoped that Serbia would reject their degrading conditions for appeasement. In fact, Austria craved it.

Without waiting for Serbia's reply, Austria called up military reserves along its borders. Americans relaxing in Austrian spas and resorts were suddenly surprised to notice the disappearance of the bellboys and waiters from their hotels and restaurants. At the height of the tourist season, bathhouses in the spas shut down for lack of personnel. So did a number of shops.

On July 26, Serbia responded to Austria's ultimatum. In a frantic effort to avoid war, Serbia agreed to almost all of Austria's humiliating demands, but Austria chose to reject Serbia's reply. Instead, the army accelerated its mobilization.

The whirlpool of war preparations spiraled outward. On the afternoon of July 26, while Nancy and Ethel blissfully shopped and packed in Venice, the

Austrian army took control of the country's railroads in order to move their men to the borders of Serbia and Russia more quickly. All regularly scheduled rail service in Austria was canceled. This convinced many American visitors to hastily pack and flee into Germany, where things were expected to be calmer.

Upon his return from the vacation in Norway, Kaiser Wilhelm was shocked by the escalation of events that had occurred during his absence. He had not imagined that all his blustering and saber rattling would trigger a war, nor did he seek to be the aggressor. When push came to shove, the kaiser wanted to draw back from the abyss of war; he hated risk-taking. The memory of his assurances of German support to Austria, given so blithely only three weeks earlier, hit him like a dash of cold water in the face.

Austria refused to listen to Germany. It was out for Serbian blood. With its army mobilized, Austria declared war on Serbia on July 28. A shudder ran through the governments of Europe, but the American tourists who vacationed in resorts, hotels, and spas remained oblivious of the horrors of war about to descend upon Europe.

The U.S. Congress barely stirred from its end-of-session lethargy. Most of the members looked forward to their summer recess and to an escape from Washington's choking summer heat. Europe's playgrounds beckoned. Many of the congressmen's families were already vacationing abroad. But none of the lawmakers was more concerned about the safety of their loved ones than Ben Johnson of Kentucky. He had never particularly liked the idea of Nancy going so far away. Now that there seemed to be a major conflict brewing in Europe, his worst nightmare had become reality. Ben hurried home and broke the war news to his wife before she read about it in the evening newspapers.

All the shades were drawn on the second floor of the White House, but it was not because of the serious news from abroad. President Woodrow Wilson had something else much more personally important on his mind. In the spring, the First Lady, Ellen, had been injured in a bad fall, and she had still not recovered her strength. On May 7, she had joined her husband in the Blue Room, where they celebrated the wedding of their younger daughter Eleanor to William McAdoo, but since that happy occasion Ellen had not been well enough to go downstairs. In the closing days of July, she grew weaker. Sitting at the bedside of his ailing beloved, Wilson told his aide, "I can think of nothing—nothing, when my dear one is suffering."[7]

On July 29 in Venice, Nancy picked up her photographs from the photo shop just off Saint Mark's Square. She had ordered an extra set of prints, not only for sending home in letters but also to share with Ethel. The women giggled over their serious-looking poses while they enjoyed a last gelato in the square.

Meanwhile, in response to Austria's declaration of war against Serbia, on July 29 Russia stationed its army on Austria's frontier to defend its small ally. For added protection in order to block a possible invasion by Austria, Russia ordered that all the bridges near its borders be destroyed. Poland, surrounded by Russia, Germany, and Austria-Hungary, called up its home guard as well. Young men, fresh from their farms, shops, and factory work, reported to their duty stations and were issued arms.

The sudden mobilization required enormous numbers of horses. Without a word of warning or offer of reimbursement, a contingent of Polish soldiers appeared at the entrance of the American Wild West show's tent outside of Warsaw and confiscated the Americans' highly trained cow ponies. The ten cowboys and dozen Indians in the cast were left without means of supporting themselves. As it turned out, there was no audience for their show anyway.

During a somber gathering of the company, the performers quickly realized how serious their predicament was. The majority of their ticket receipts had been cabled back to the States, leaving them with barely enough money to maintain themselves. The men were in for another nasty shock when they tried to draw extra funds on their credit. The Polish banks, husbanding their supply of hard cash against an unknown financial future, refused to honor a piece of paper drawn on an unknown American bank. The performers were stuck with whatever change they had in their pockets. Furthermore, they knew that the last train out of Warsaw would leave that evening. If they were ever going to get back home, it was now or never.

Reluctantly, the Americans came to the only solution they thought was possible. They abandoned their tent and props and left a note to their hotel proprietor telling him that he was now the proud owner of a perfectly good tent, as well as most of their baggage in lieu of payment for their rooms. Then the cowboys and Indians stole out of the hotel wearing the only things of value that they owned—their expensive, colorful costumes. At the train station, they spent the rest of their remaining money on rail tickets to Hamburg, then they squeezed themselves onto the train that was filled with other panicked tourists.[8] Of all the Americans who fled Europe that week, the Wild West show cast members were probably the most unusually dressed.

On July 30, the web of European alliances tightened into a stranglehold. In particular, Italy found itself in an uncomfortable spot. In 1882, the Italian government had signed an agreement of mutual protection with Germany and Austria-Hungary. Known as the Triple Alliance, the three countries pledged to come to the aid of each other should one be attacked. In short, it was a defensive pact. Now Germany and Austria-Hungary expected their neighbor to join them in the coming fight. The Italians had no desire to honor their agreement.

Clearly Italy's allies were the aggressors, not the defenders. Germany mobilized and expected Italy to attack the southern border of France, but Italy did nothing. The French held their breath, hoping that Italy would declare itself neutral.

By the morning of July 31, tensions mounted in the capitals of the five Great Powers. Germany sent an ultimatum to Russia, ordering that country to demobilize within twelve hours.

Russia chose to ignore Germany. With its army spread out over its vast country and handicapped by a primitive transportation system, it would take weeks before the Russian army could be up to strength on its western border. Who knew what would happen in the intervening time? In any eventuality, Russia intended to be prepared.

Germany also sent an ultimatum to France that ordered it to stay neutral, even if Russia then joined Serbia against Austria. Faced with a possible war on two fronts—France on the west and Russia on the east—Kaiser Wilhelm was perplexed and anxious. If France chose to fight, he wondered what its ally England would do.

In London, the British cabinet was divided on the action they should take if a war broke out between France and Germany. The majority of the cabinet wanted to stand aside and let the Continent tear itself apart.

Standing aside was not a viable option for France. The French military commanders realized that if Germany attacked France, the invaders would probably march through the flat lands of Flanders. As the hostilities escalated, the French government knew that Germany, bent on conquering its old enemy France, would initiate the attack.

But France must not be seen as the aggressor, no matter how badly the French desired the conflict. In the eyes of the watching world, France's role must appear to be entirely defensive. Lest any nervous French soldier on the Belgian frontier literally jump over the line, France withdrew its forces ten kilometers from the border and forbade anyone to go nearer. The French army waited. The next move was up to Germany. Europe had become a vast game of chess.

With no reply to its ultimatums, Germany reexperienced its old anxiety about being encircled by hostile powers. In a speech from his balcony to the citizens of Berlin, the kaiser announced that the "sword has been forced into our hand."[9] The chief of the general staff, General Moltke, implemented the Schlieffen Plan. It was the moment that Moltke had been preparing for since 1906. Der Tag ("the day") would be tomorrow, August 1, 1914.

Meanwhile, on a sunny July 31, Nancy and Ethel bade their final farewells to Venice. Then, with Daisy Carroll and the gallant Mr. Laugieri, plus a carload of baggage including Nancy's twenty-six pieces of luggage, the women boarded the Milan-bound train. Tonight, the excited party would sleep in Switzerland. They did not have a care in the world.

That same evening in Venice, Nicholas Butler stood on the balcony of his hotel room with his family and listened to the nightly serenade, which floated up from the water. "The Grand Canal, swarming with gondolas carrying musicians and singers to serenade the guests of the hotels looked as safe as Coney Island," he recalled.[10]

On that last night of peace in Europe, the Butlers were serenaded in Venice. The Vanderbilts slept soundly in Cortina. RAC Smith and his family enjoyed a dinner with friends in Bozen, and Nancy and Ethel arrived at their hotel in Lausanne, Switzerland. None of these American tourists had the slightest notion that within the next twenty-four hours their cozy world of pleasure and privilege would be shattered forever. Even if they had suspected that something was amiss, they could have done nothing.

In that final hour of the Gilded Age, these wealthy, privileged members of America's elite arrogantly presumed that their nationality was their shield; that their letters of credit and introduction were all the protection that they needed no matter what those "furriners" might do to each other. It took the guns of August to scare the literal wits out of them and to blast the world into the twentieth century.

CHAPTER 7

"A madman wants to change the map"

Saturday, August 1, 1914—*Der Tag* dawned hot and sunny. It was the day that General Moltke, chief of the German general staff, had dreamed about since he had inherited the Schlieffen Plan from his predecessor in 1906. Conceived in 1899 by General Count von Schlieffen, Germany's blueprint for war against France had been fine-tuned for the next six years until his retirement.[1] In turn Moltke had refined and revised the plan for eight more years. Now the day had finally arrived. Six weeks from now Moltke expected to dine in Paris.

The German ultimatum to Russia expired at noon on August 1. At five o'clock in the afternoon, Germany declared war on Russia. In Berlin, when the crowds around the kaiser's palace were informed that they were now officially at war, the people spontaneously broke into singing the hymn "Now Thank We All Our God." The order for general mobilization went out over the wires.

Even before Germany's formal declaration of war, a change had already swept across the Continent. Nicholas Butler noticed it immediately on the morning of August 1 in Venice. "In twelve hours this state of calm was changed into one of absolute chaos," he later remarked.[2]

Butler, alarmed over the disintegrating political situation, decided that he and his family would leave Venice and return to Paris as quickly as possible. Butler, his wife, daughter, and three friends left Venice, picked up their automobile on the mainland side of the lagoon, and were soon motoring through the northern Italian countryside where the grapes hung heavy from their vines, waiting to be harvested. They reached Milan by nightfall.

After spending Friday night in a hotel in Lausanne, Nancy, Ethel, Daisy Carroll, and Mr. Laugieri noticed the tension in the air when they awoke from their pleasant sleep on Saturday morning, August 1. They quickly learned that Switzerland was preparing for war.

"I felt such pity for the men who had to quit their wives and families and occupations because in a far-off land a maniac had killed an archduke who meant nothing to them. One could see that they had no interest in the fight," Nancy later recalled.

"A waiter in our hotel came in to serve tea, upset with suppressed [sic] emotion. I remarked that he looked unwell. He replied with terrible bitterness, 'Madam, I am aflame inside. After I have served you this afternoon, I must go to war, not because we have been wronged, not for our liberty, but because a madman wants to change the map. For this insane idea we must give up our lives.'"[3]

Daisy Carroll's discomfort increased a hundredfold when Mr. Laugieri returned from the railway station with the news that France had closed its borders and was mobilizing its men. According to the stationmaster, Germany was preparing to declare war on Russia, France, and perhaps even England—who knew?

Daisy Carroll knew exactly what they should do—return to Venice immediately. As the American consul, her husband would be the two young women's best adviser. Nancy could not believe the situation was as bad as it sounded. Yesterday everything was perfectly normal. How could it have changed overnight? What did a mere stationmaster know? Nancy wanted to stay put and see what happened. Daisy Carroll became insistent. They would return to Venice at once.

The trip from the hotel to the train depot proved more difficult than Nancy and her party had expected. "All the horses in Lausanne had disappeared. We tried all day to get our baggage to the station but we could find no conveyance. After we had given up all hope of ever getting it to the train, our courier appeared with what he said was the last horse in the city, an old beast, too decrepit for military service. This poor creature pulled our trunks to the station, while we women walked, for we absolutely could not get a carriage."[4]

Having been in Switzerland for less than twenty-four hours, Nancy, Ethel, Daisy Carroll, and Mr. Laugieri boarded the southbound train and retraced their route to Milan. As the miles clicked away beneath her, Nancy suppressed her extreme disappointment, and she managed to keep the Johnson temper in check. It was only a tempest in a teapot, she thought. By this time next week, everything would be back to normal. This retreat to Venice was nothing but a waste of money.

One person who did remain in Lausanne on August 1 was Dartmouth student Arno Behnke. "Today is the Swiss mid-summer patriotic day," he noted in his pocket diary, "but for the first time in many hundreds of years—somebody said 633—it was not celebrated. All the fetes planned for the day were abruptly abandoned, because word had gone out that the army must mobilize. Crowds of men surrounded government placards everywhere learning where they were to report. I went into a confectionery shop to buy some candy. The old Swiss woman who waited on me said as she sold me some little red ices each of which was decorated with a white cross, 'This is the only celebration we can have today.'"[5]

Meanwhile, in Berlin, the kaiser was not a happy man. "We have run our heads into the noose," he scribbled in the margin of one of the telegrams he received that day. Grasping at straws, the kaiser called Moltke and ordered him to deploy the troops on one frontier only—Russia. The chief of staff dug in his heels. The Schlieffen Plan called for a two-front war; first attack France while its cumbersome ally organized its army, then attack Russia. Even as he argued with the kaiser, one-and-a-half-million men were marching toward Belgium.

"Your Majesty," said Moltke through clenched teeth, "it cannot be done. The deployment of millions cannot be improvised." After making a few more points in favor of attacking France, the general added the ultimate German reason for everything: "It cannot be altered."

"Your uncle," replied Wilhelm, referring to the victorious field marshal of the Franco-Prussian War, "would have given me a different answer." By now sweating under his heavy tunic, Moltke refused to back down. He knew that the first German regiment would be crossing into neutral Luxembourg within the hour.[6]

The kaiser, fearful of what the English would do if Luxembourg were violated, telephoned his order for the soldiers to be stopped. In his memoirs, Moltke wrote, "At that moment, I thought my heart would break." When his aide brought him the written order canceling the march into Luxembourg, Moltke threw down his pen and refused to sign.[7]

The kaiser's telephoned message was too late. At 7 p.m. on August 1, exactly in accordance with the initial part of the Schlieffen Plan, the lead company of the German 69th Infantry Regiment, under the command of a young lieutenant, arrived at the Luxembourg border. Waiting for him was the bravest and most gallant woman in Europe on that chaotic day, Princess Marie Adelaide, Grand Duchess of Luxembourg.[8]

Princess Marie had been allowed to assume the Luxembourg crown after the death of her father, William, who had died in 1912 without a male heir. She was the first female ruler of this small principality and was a mere twenty years old when she faced down the German invaders of her country.[9] In the early evening of this first day of war, Marie had her chauffeur straddle her large black automobile across the center of the bridge that led into her country. Sitting in the rear seat, looking regal in her pearls, the grand duchess stared down her nose at the Germans.

The lieutenant got out of his car and strode over to the young ruler. Using rough language, he ordered her to go back to her home and let them pass. Her Royal Highness refused while her chauffeur and lady-in-waiting trembled.

The German officer became rattled. The grand duchess's personal resistance was not one of the contingencies covered in the Schlieffen Plan. Yet the lieutenant knew he could not back down. His entire regiment behind him watched every move of the drama being played out on the bridge. The plan ordered that any resistance must be met with reprisals. The lieutenant drew his revolver. With as steady a hand as he could manage, he pointed it directly at Princess Marie Adelaide and again ordered her to move.

The grand duchess regarded him for a long moment, then she stared at the gun. With a slight nod of her head, she acquiesced to the rude officer's demands. In a clear voice so that the bystanders at both ends of the bridge could hear her, she replied that, under duress, she was unable to resist the German invasion. The lieutenant breathed a little easier. He had no desire to spill royal blood. But the princess added that she intended to telegraph her displeasure to the kaiser himself. Then she gave her chauffeur the signal to start his engine.[10]

Bloodshed had been averted, but Les Trois Vierges—the Three Virgins of Faith, Hope, and Charity—were irrevocably violated. Germany had literally crossed the line.

Across the Atlantic, a few far-seeing men realized that the German threat was more than "a tempest in a teapot," as Nancy Johnson suspected. A young politician serving as assistant secretary of the navy, Franklin Delano Roosevelt, heard the news of the European mobilization while riding on a train to Reading, Pennsylvania. That evening he wrote to his wife, Eleanor, "A complete smash up is inevitable. It will be the greatest war in the world's history."[11]

CHAPTER 8

"It is a king's war"

The change from peacetime to war was sudden, swift, and inexplicable in its meaning for the great majority of the people in Europe, both natives and tourists alike. Friday, July 31, was filled with picnics, sightseeing, pleasure boating, and the beginning of the harvest season in the grain-ripe fields. On Saturday, August 1, the borders shut like steel vault doors, mobilization began, banks refused to grant credit, and chaos reigned.

Sunday morning, August 2, was the scene of more Swiss patriotism, as Arno Behnke noted in his diary:

> The bulletin boards are still the centers of excited groups. Soldiers hurried through the Place St. Francois all day, and every man not in uniform wore a little Swiss flag. The pigeons fluttered as usual above the vivid flowers clustered about the church entrance, but no one noticed them. The old grey edifice was crowded to the vestibule and the tremendous volume which issued from all these throats when they sang that cry of a troubled and defenseless human soul "A Mighty Fortress is our God, a bulwark never yielding" sounded far across the Square. The good pastor, an eloquent man, besought the people to be "strong and of good courage."[1]

Germany, Russia, France, and Austria-Hungary armed for war. Switzerland prepared its defenses. Italy wavered, leaning toward neutrality. Finally, late on August 1, Italy escaped through a loophole in its alliance pact with Germany and Austria-Hungary and declared its neutrality. Germany immediately denounced its erstwhile ally as a traitor.

On Sunday morning, August 2, Pope Pius X issued an international plea for peace.

> At this moment, when nearly the whole of Europe is being dragged into the vortex of a most terrible war, with its present dangers and miseries and

consequences to follow, the very thought of which must strike everyone with grief and horror, we whose care is the life and welfare of so many citizens and peoples cannot but be deeply moved and our heart wrung with bitterest sorrow.

And in the midst of this universal confusion and peril we feel and know that both Fatherly love and the Apostolic ministry demand of us that we should with all earnestness turn the thoughts of Christendom thither "whence cometh help"—to Christ, the Prince of Peace, and the most powerful mediator between God and man.

We charge, therefore, the Catholics of the whole world to approach the throne of Grace and Mercy, each and all of them, and more especially the clergy, whose duty furthermore it will be to make in every parish, as their Bishops shall direct, public supplication so that the merciful God may, as it were, be wearied with the prayers of His children and speedily remove the evil causes of war, giving to them who rule to think thoughts of peace and not of affliction.[2]

Germany and Austria ignored the tired old man who sat in the Chair of Peter. With its troops now occupying Luxembourg according to the Schlieffen Plan's schedule, Germany next turned its attention to Belgium—the pathway to France. The Germans delivered an ultimatum to the Belgian government, saying, in effect, that Germany was forced to enter Belgium—and violate that country's precious neutrality—in order to "defend itself" against a French invasion. As ludicrous as this twisted logic may have sounded, Germany's intention was deadly serious, and King Albert of the Belgians knew it.

To the German high command, their ultimatum was a mere formality. They had never taken that little country seriously. Belgium's tiny army was the stuff of comic operettas—chocolate soldiers who looked dashing in drawing rooms but who would run at the first sound of gunfire. Furthermore, the Belgians were a practical people—they would stand aside and allow the German army to march though their country rather than suffer the bloodshed, pillage, and famine that would be part of German reprisals.

Count von Schlieffen had miscalculated an important point in his plan. Though the Belgian people were peace loving, they were also fiercely proud. For over seventy years, Belgium's powerful neighbors had observed its hard-won neutral status. Nothing would induce Belgium to jeopardize its own position that had brought such prosperity to its people. Its "chocolate-soldier army" was far from cowardly; they existed as only a home guard. To allow either France or Germany to invade the other through Belgium's territory unimpeded would violate everything the Belgians held sacred. The brash

ultimatum, in effect, demanded that Belgium ally itself with Germany against
France.

At 9 P.M. on August 2, King Albert met with his Council of State. "Our
answer must be 'No' whatever the consequences. Our duty is to defend our ter-
ritorial integrity. In this we must not fail."[3]

The majority of statesman in Europe and across the Atlantic did not believe that the Germans would dare to carry out their threat. To do so would
trigger a full-scale war and would draw the Fifth Power, England, into the fray.
In Washington, the State Department, prodded by hundreds of anxious telegrams, telephone calls, and worried visitors like Representative Ben Johnson,
was much more concerned with rescuing the Americans stranded "over there"
than with the illogical possibility that Germany might invade Belgium. One
early action that the U.S. State Department considered was sending military
transports to Europe to bring home their countrymen and women.

At least one reader of the *New York Times* had already grasped the precari-
ous situation of the Americans caught abroad. William Volz wrote an impas-
sioned letter to the editor:

> In view of the cancellation of steamship sailings, both here and abroad,
> with thousands of Americans now in Europe unable to book passage for
> returning to the States, it would seem that this Government should take a
> hand in the matter, and utilize the army transports now under supervision
> of the Quartermaster's Department for this purpose.
>
> Some of these vessels were regular passenger steamers of large tonnage
> before being taken over by the Government during the Spanish War, and
> would be well adapted for such service. The writer deems it the duty of this
> Government to provide the necessary facilities in such a case for the return
> of our citizens who may be held up by the present deplorable conditions
> in Europe, as was recently done during the Mexican troubles in Vera Cruz,
> at which time the Government chartered several steamers for this purpose,
> besides sending a number home on vessels of war.
> William E. Volz, New York, Aug. 1, 1914[4]

While most of official Washington was closed in observance of Sunday, at
least one American official in Europe did not wait for the result of the State
Department's ponderous decision-making process. On August 2, acting on his
own volition, Consul General John Edward Jones in Genoa began negotiations
with officials from the Lloyd Sabaudo Line[5] to charter one of its smaller steamers, the *Re d'Italia*,[6] which currently rode at anchor in Genoa's harbor. At the
outbreak of hostilities, practically all of the steamship companies in Europe,

including the ones in neutral Italy, had canceled all their sailings until further notice. By late afternoon of August 2, rumors were already circulating around the Genoa seaport that the Germans had mined the entrance to the harbor and that German submarines lurked in the Mediterranean waiting for unsuspecting prey. The steamship companies had no desire to hazard their vessels or passengers.

Jones persisted. The Lloyd Sabaudo officials put the price of a first-class berth on the *Re d'Italia* at 500 francs[7] to be paid in cash and in advance. Jones telegraphed the consular offices throughout Italy that he had a New York–bound steamer sailing from Genoa on Tuesday, August 11. Americans who heard the news through the consular grapevines hurried toward Genoa.

On August 2, RAC Smith had finally arrived in Venice, and he went immediately to the U.S. consulate, where he found B. Harvey Carroll besieged by panicked Americans clamoring to go home. Many of the hotels and restaurants in Venice had refused to accept foreign personal checks in lieu of payment; the proprietors wanted cash. With only the spare change in their handbags and wallets, the American tourists found themselves in dire financial straits—many of them for the first time in their wealthy lives. Faced with this virtual poverty, many panicked and expected their beleaguered consuls and ambassadors to pay their bills.

In May 1914, when B. Harvey Carroll had accepted his posting to Venice, he envisioned several delightful years in the midst of the most unique city in the world. Though the crisis of the widowed bride had been unpleasant, it paled in comparison to the growing problems that he now faced. While coping with hysterical, demanding countrymen and women, he also worried about the safety of his wife and the two young women with her who were now somewhere in Switzerland. He had already received a cable from the State Department in Washington inquiring about the welfare of Nancy Johnson, the personal friend of the president.

RAC Smith was not unduly alarmed that Sunday afternoon. Though he had only ten dollars on his person, he was sure that he would be able to draw out more funds on Monday morning when the banks opened. At the moment he was more interested in the news of the *Re d'Italia*'s sailing. He was determined that he and his family would be on it. Tomorrow, the Smiths planned to take the train to Milan and from there to Genoa.

Meanwhile, early Sunday morning Nicholas Butler and his party of five drove out of Milan and headed north toward Switzerland. They intended to reach Lausanne by nightfall. Very quickly, however, they were disconcerted to find the roads choked by "masses of cavalry and artillery moving north."

Though Italy was expected to declare its neutrality at any moment, nevertheless the government stationed troops along the border.

Unable to drive up the crowded road, the Butlers managed to turn their car
around and go back to Milan. Once in that city, the party abandoned their
automobile and boarded a train bound for Paris. As their train rolled out of
the station, Butler wiped his face with his handkerchief and told the others
that it would be smooth going from now on.

The university president spoke too soon. When the conductor poked his
head into their compartment to check their tickets, he informed the stunned
Americans that the French borders were closed and that the train would not
be going to Paris. He suggested that the Americans get off at Lausanne, near
the Swiss-French border, and hope for the best. Although frustrated by this
news, the Butlers decided to take the conductor's advice.

The trip was much slower than usual as the train was shunted onto sidings
to make way for troop trains headed for the border. Tired and feeling gritty
from a day of heat and cinders, the Butlers and their friends alighted in Lausanne at one o'clock in the morning on Monday, August 3. There were no baggage attendants on the platform. In fact, there was no one else there except a
few other befuddled passengers. Butler was forced to unload their trunks himself from the baggage car—an unusual chore for the president of Columbia
University.

Another nasty surprise awaited them when they finally arrived at the Hotel
Cecil. The place was filled to overflowing with Americans who had fled from
France. The best the hotel manager could do was to offer the Butler women
blankets and sofas in one of the public rooms. Butler was allotted a bathtub.
Though its dimensions did not fit the portly gentleman, he fell asleep imme-
diately, exhausted by the strains of the past twenty-four hours.[8]

Earlier on August 2, Nancy and her party arrived back in Milan about the
same time that the Butlers headed up the same tracks to Lausanne. At this
point in Nancy's journey, Mr. Laugieri parted with them in order to return to
Genoa as quickly as possible. He knew that the consul general would need all
the help he could get. Daisy Carroll and Nancy and Ethel pressed on to Venice,
finally arriving at the American consulate after nightfall. The sight that greeted
them there filled the women with dismay. The consulate "was full of people,"
Nancy observed with shock. B. Harvey Carroll "allowed them to sleep on the
floors, and he turned some of the rooms into regular eating places. He did all
kinds of unselfish things, going much further than his government would have
requested him to do."[9]

Nancy and Ethel's room, which they had only vacated some thirty-six hours
earlier, was now in use by others who were in more distress than they. Daisy

Carroll set the two up in a much smaller accommodation, where they fell asleep surrounded by their piles of luggage.

Monday, August 3, brought more anxiety across Europe. The defiant Belgian "No!" thrilled and surprised many, both statesmen and ordinary people alike. The British Admiralty issued orders to the Royal Navy to prepare for coastal defense. In order for German High Seas Fleet warships to reach France, they would have to pass through the North Sea and the Channel. The British Parliament wondered if Germany would invade Belgium. If so, Great Britain would be forced to take a stand against the aggressor. The honor of its protection agreement with Belgium demanded it.

On the morning of August 3, the banks did not open for business in London, much to the consternation of the populace. The American tourists particularly found themselves without a cent in their pockets to pay for hotel bills or, more important, transportation back to the States. As a favor for a friend in the U.S. embassy in London, Herbert Hoover volunteered his time and organizational expertise to help his stranded, frightened compatriots. Hoover marked his fortieth birthday while working long into the night for the American Citizens Relief Committee, "getting the busted Yankee safely home." Looking back on his service in London during that first week of World War I, Hoover remarked, "I did not realize it at that moment, but on this Monday [August 3, 1914] my engineering career was over. I was on the slippery slope of public life."[10]

The Italian government also closed all the banks in the country on August 3. When RAC Smith went to cash his check, he had a nasty jolt of reality. "I had exactly $10.00 when I arrived in Venice and did not worry, because I thought I would be able to draw all I needed at the bank the next morning [Monday, August 3]. To my surprise I found that the banks were all closed and I could not obtain any money anywhere. Fortunately, I had an Italian friend in Florence, who sent me 10,000 lire by messenger in answer to my telegram informing him of my situation. This enabled me to go to Genoa, and also to assist some Americans who were entirely without funds."[11]

On Monday morning, Nancy received the first in a series of telegrams from Mr. Laugieri, who had lost no time in acting on her behalf in Genoa. "ADVISE LEAVE EUROPE IMMEDIATELY ON STEAMER RE ITALIA [sic] SAILING GENOA ELEVENTH INSTANT FOR NEW YORK WITH GREATEST DIFFICULTY OBTAINED FROM COMMANDER FRIEND OF MINE KEEP LAST TWO BERTHS FOR YOU TILL TOMORROW MORNING 500 FRANCS[12] EACH WIRE REPLY CONSULATE LAUGIERI."[13]

Nancy replied immediately, confirming their berths, and she asked if there was a cabin for Daisy Carroll. Seeing the distress of so many of his compatriots firsthand, B. Harvey Carroll had decided it would be better for Daisy to return to the safety of the United States.

When Nancy and Ethel went out to cash their bank drafts to pay for the steamer tickets, they, too, discovered that all the banks had closed. Earlier, on July 30, Nancy and Ethel had chosen not to cash their checks before leaving for Paris because they did not want to travel with large sums of money. In Nancy's letter to her father on July 16, she had told him that she would have twenty dollars in cash left at the end of the month. Since that time, she had to pay for her unexpected return trip to Venice from Lausanne. She now had very little change left in her purse. She had no idea how she would be able to pay for her ship passage.[14] For the first time in her life, Nancy Johnson experienced the financial insecurity that constantly dogged most Americans. She did not like the feeling at all.

Stuck in Lausanne, Nicholas Butler also found himself in reduced circumstances. Early on the morning of August 3, he returned to the Lausanne station in the hope of purchasing tickets for Paris. There he met a "grizzled veteran of the Franco-Prussian war" who now worked for the Swiss railway. When Butler asked the man if he would have to serve at the front, the old soldier replied, "No, I am too old. I am seventy-two; but my four boys went yesterday, God help them! And I hate to have them go, for, sir," he lowered his voice, "this is not a people's war; it is a king's war. And when it is over there may not be so many kings," he added with a glint in his eye.[15]

Butler again asked if the French border was really closed. The old man assured him that it was; there was no chance of anyone going to Paris from Switzerland in the foreseeable future. When Butler asked to buy tickets for Milan, the man again shook his head. Impossible, the only passengers that would be on the Milan train were the Italian guest workers who were being sent back home from French fields and vineyards.

Nicholas Butler was not used to being told "no." While he pondered his next question, his gaze roved around the deserted station. On a siding he spied a railway car marked "Reserved." He pointed to it and asked what the car was reserved for. "Public officials," the old man replied.

Was anyone using it today? Butler asked as a thoroughly audacious plan formed in his mind. When the Swiss railway man replied with a guarded "no," Butler seized the moment.

"Very well. Let's loosen the brake and bring it down the track."

When the alarmed railway employee asked why, Butler replied, "I'll show you."

The old soldier and the university president managed to release the brake. The car rolled gently down the track, where they halted it at the best spot for a hookup. Then Butler retrieved his baggage from the station's storeroom and loaded it inside the car. After that exertion, Columbia's president raced back to the hotel and hustled the rest of his party to the station with hurried words of explanation.

When the southbound train pulled into the Lausanne station at 8:15 A.M., Butler boldly stepped up to the train's conductor, pointed to the waiting VIP car, and said in his most pompous French, "This is the special reserved car that you had instructions to take back with you to Milan."

His ploy worked. The conductor raised his hat and told the engineer to connect the purloined car to the rear of the train. Five minutes later the Butler party were on their way back to Milan. As he relaxed against the plush seat of the luxurious car, Butler wondered if there would be hell to pay later for this piece of highhanded theft.[16]

While other Americans, like Nancy and the Butlers, hastened to leave Lausanne, Arno Behnke was still at his hotel on August 3, though he, too, noticed more signs of the developing war.

> Our waiters are all leaving. Some of them do not want to go at all. One said this noon with terrible emphasis, "This is a war of Emperors and the Emperors will hear from us after it is over."
>
> The proprietor has changed our menus; we have been put on reduced rations. They say that the food supply of Switzerland is not sufficient to provide for the people if the country passes through a long period of isolation.
>
> My tailor said today that he was going to close, since both his customers and his workmen have all left. I did not think that the war would affect even the tailors in less than a week.[17]

In Washington, D.C., President Wilson arose from his dying wife's bedside to hold a press conference. "America stands ready to help the rest of the world," he told the jostling reporters. The United States "could reap a great permanent glory out of doing it."[18] The president saw the United States' peaceful neutrality as the opportunity to play a greater role in world affairs at the conclusion of the war—a war he expected to be short-lived. America would become the world's peacekeeper.

Reading the newspapers about the outbreak of hostilities in Europe, the citizens of the United States collectively sighed and thought, "Thank God it's *over there!*" The clash of the European nations had little impact on the people of New York, Philadelphia, Baltimore, or Chicago. However, it was a far different situation for their stranded countrymen and women who now found themselves between the proverbial rock and a hard place. The harried

American consuls across Europe flooded the State Department with urgent cables for help. As the European political situation worsened with each passing hour, the American diplomats were besieged by their desperate—and at times—hysterical countrymen and women eager to get back home. The American diplomatic community in the beleaguered countries rose to the occasion and coped with a crisis of growing proportions for which nothing had prepared them. It was, as one put it, "the most terrible August in the history of the world."[19]

At 6:15 on the evening of August 3, the French learned that Germany had declared war on their country. The pace of mobilization escalated—and so did the tension. As the twilight of August 3 darkened London's sky, the British cabinet waited tensely to see if Germany would really violate Belgium's neutrality. Sir Edward Gray, the British foreign secretary, watched the streetlamps being lit outside Whitehall. To a nearby colleague, he remarked, "The lights are going out all over Europe."[20]

In Berlin, Ambassador James W. Gerard and his wife devoted themselves to soothing their compatriots' fears as they expedited their return to the States. The paperwork and red tape created by the German bureaucracy were staggering. All persons leaving Germany had to present passports from their embassies. This was at a time when passports were not generally required for the recreational traveler. To complicate an already difficult situation, Gerard not only represented the United States but also the interests of Russia, since that country had now broken off all formal diplomatic relations with Germany.

"We issued 418 passports today," wrote Joseph C. Grew, the secretary at the U.S. embassy in Berlin on August 3. "All very tired—I have lost four pounds in three days. . . . Telegrams come in every minute from Americans in all parts of Germany, asking for help, some of them hysterical."[21]

One American politician in Washington, D.C., paid special attention to the mounting number of cables that poured into the State Department from the consulates across the Atlantic. Speaker of the House "Champ" Clark decided to recall Congress from its summer recess, which had just begun that weekend. Perhaps he was motivated by the anxiety of his good friend and colleague Ben Johnson, who had grown more concerned about his daughter's safety with each passing hour.

Despite Clark's urgent call to the House members, few heeded the Speaker. The situation in Europe did not appear to be particularly dangerous to the absent representatives, certainly not enough to forego an afternoon of fishing. Out of patience, Clark issued a thundering ultimatum to his recalcitrant lawmakers: return at once to Capitol Hill or suffer the indignity of being arrested by the House sergeant of arms and to have U.S. marshals forcibly return them to their seats. The trudge up the Hill became a stampede by the truant members of the House.

In the midafternoon of August 3, while Nancy, RAC Smith, and Nicholas Butler attempted to cash their checks in Italy, the joint session of the House and Senate of the U.S. Congress unanimously voted to authorize the expenditure of $250,000 to aid the penniless American tourists abroad. This allotted sum seemed enormous, but the State Department made it very clear to President Wilson that it would not be nearly enough. The State Department officials contended that the situation abroad was considerably more serious than anyone could have imagined only two days earlier. Members of Congress voted an additional $2 million. Then they debated the quickest way to get the money across the ocean.

In 1914 electronic deposits and wire transfers by computers were inconceivable financial services. Under the complex financial system of the time, money cabled from America had to go through the Bank of England in London before the funds could be forwarded to another European country. This system usually worked—in peacetime. Now the war had effectively shut down borders and frozen assets in the banks across Europe.

England further complicated the matter by implementing a strict censorship over its communication lines. American banks used a variety of identifying codes and numbers when cabling transactions abroad. In these unsettled times, all such incoming codes were considered suspect and were not forwarded by the censor office. Money cabled from New York for a depositor in Paris never got past the British censorship, but languished in fiscal limbo for an indefinite period. It took several days of precious time before this bottleneck became apparent to the State Department. Meanwhile the horde of suddenly destitute Americans in Europe had swelled almost beyond control.

By late afternoon on the third day of August, help was finally on the way in the shape of a semiretired U.S. Navy ship based in New York City, the USS *Tennessee,* an armored cruiser that had been commissioned in 1904. The ship had sixteen boilers and could carry a full load of nine hundred tons of coal. Its fastest speed was twenty-two knots; however, since the beginning of 1914 the *Tennessee* had been acting as a floating barracks in the Brooklyn Navy Yard in New York City. On the evening of August 3, its skipper was enjoying some shore leave in Boston when he received an urgent message to report immediately back to his ship.

Captain Benton C. Decker, a member of the U.S. Naval Academy's class of 1887, was no stranger to responding to calls for help. In his twenty-seven years of service in the U.S. Navy, he had already been a part of two famous rescue operations. During the Spanish-American War, young Lieutenant Decker successfully extracted seventeen Spanish crewmen from their burning naval vessels following the battle of Santiago, Cuba, on July 3, 1898. Decker's compassion and bravery were highly commended in dispatches. More recently, in April 1912 Commander Decker, commanding officer of the scout cruiser USS *Chester*, took part in the unsuccessful search for survivors or bodies from the *Titanic* disaster. Now, in 1914, Captain Decker was once again called to the rescue. He was about to undertake the most unusual assignment of his career.

As the captain hurried down to New York from Boston, a makeshift crew was already being gathered from other navy ships present at the Brooklyn Navy Yard. The *Tennessee*'s usual complement numbered 860 men, but the navy could only round up 700 sailors on such short notice. The call for additional men went out to all the Atlantic Coast naval stations. Lieutenant Commander E. P. Jessop, commander of the torpedo boat USS *Benham*, suddenly found himself ordered to the *Tennessee* as its executive officer pro tem. Shortly after midnight on August 4, a detachment of Marines reported for guard duty. The mystery surrounding the *Tennessee*'s special mission deepened.

By August 4, Ambassador James Gerard in Berlin literally felt the strain.[1] In a single twenty-four-hour period, he signed over a thousand passports, giving him a severe case of writer's cramp. For one special group of Americans he had to go much further.

At the end of July, one of the touring Wild West shows had been performing in Berlin. When war was declared, the Onondaga Indians,[2] who made up half the performers, were immediately interned in a German prison "for their own protection" while the cowboys were sent from Berlin toward the seacoast.

The Onondaga are one of the six tribes that make up the proud Iroquois Confederation. In 1914 all Native Americans, including the Onondaga, fell into a vague limbo of nationality. Officially American Indians were not considered citizens of the United States, but members of their own sovereign tribes. Among the Iroquois, the Onondaga have been traditionally known as the Peacekeepers of the Council Fire. Over the next few days, these proud men were beaten and humiliated by their guards. No thanks to the popularity of the Wild West shows and cheap western novels, the Germans nursed a stereotype image of the American "Red Indians" as savages, and they considered the Onondaga to be highly dangerous to civilized society. The idea that these "red men" were "loose" in their country terrified the xenophobic Germans.[3]

Gerard worked his way through a seeming labyrinth of red tape before he could finally free the young men and send them back to the States. After the Onondaga returned to their reservation in upstate New York, the Iroquois tribal elders met in council. In retaliation for the insults suffered by the peace-loving Onondaga, the Iroquois immediately issued a formal declaration of war against Germany in the fall of 1914.[4] They were the first nation in the Western Hemisphere to do so.[5]

Unlike Gerard, Ambassador Myron Herrick in Paris had a great many more people to cope with as American tourists poured into Paris seeking immediate help. Many of these tourists were the same ones that Ambassador Gerard had sent out of Germany. As the days and nights fused into an exhausted blur for Herrick and his staff, the demands for instant money and train transportation grew even more strident. Both commodities were in very short supply in Paris.

Of all the U.S. representatives in Europe, Walter Haines Page, ambassador to England's Court of Saint James, was the hardest pressed. More than his colleagues in Berlin and Paris, Page had ample opportunity to experience the ugly side of his compatriots.

The first few days of August were chaotic at the embassy, as panicked Americans flooded into London from all over Europe. Page went for three days without a spare moment to take a bath, and he snatched sleep in fitful catnaps. By August 4, his nerves were strained to the breaking point.

When a powerful U.S. senator in Washington wired him: "Send my wife and daughter home on the first ship," the frazzled ambassador nearly lost his usual composure. After a three-day search by embassy staff members who were urgently needed elsewhere, the senator's family were finally located "sitting in a swell hotel waiting for me to bring them stateroom tickets on a silver tray!" Page recalled.[6]

Meanwhile, across the English Channel, Germany took the step that would eventually doom it to defeat and the loss of its empire. At two minutes past 8 A.M. on August 4, the first German regiment crossed the Belgian frontier at Gemmerich, thirty miles from Liege. The Belgian border guards met them with a brave but brief resistance. German Chief of Staff Moltke hoped that these first few shots were fired merely for honor's sake and that Belgium would "come to an understanding" with the superior force that now marched down its roads. For this reason, Germany had not declared war on the little country even as thousands of German soldiers drove deeper into the countryside. The world's reaction to this shocking violation of Belgium's neutrality was immediate. Germany was vilified.

Though rain poured down on Berlin on August 4, the mood in that city was anything but gloomy. Speaking to the members of the Reichstag, Chancellor Theobold von Bethmann-Hollweg crowed, "Whatever our lot may be, August 4, 1914, will remain for all eternity one of Germany's greatest days!"[7] Years after the war, the German crown prince rued "our greatest disaster." August 4, 1914, was the day "when we Germans lost the first great battle in the eyes of the world."[8]

Ecstatic crowds in Rome cheered the announcement of Italy's neutrality. Pope Pius X prayed for a swift end to the madness. Now that its southern border no longer needed protection, France was able to redeploy the troops that had been assigned there only a few days earlier. Four divisions of French soldiers took trains north toward the Ardennes Mountains, where the French high command prepared to launch their counterattack against Germany—the ill-conceived Plan 17.

The British Parliament dispatched an ultimatum to Germany, stating that Britain felt honor bound to uphold Belgium's neutrality and that Britain expected Germany to understand that commitment and withdraw. The ultimatum was, in fact, tantamount to a declaration of war.

When the British ambassador in Berlin presented the ultimatum to the chancellor, Bethmann threw a tantrum. In a near-hysterical harangue, Bethmann shouted at the stunned Englishman that whatever course the war might take in the future, the destruction would be Britain's fault "all for just a word—'neutrality'—just for a scrap of paper."[9]

The kaiser took it more personally. He thought that the British ultimatum was an act of deepest betrayal. He simply could not believe that England was going to step into the fray and take up arms against them for the sake of a weak little country like Belgium.

Midnight came and went with nothing heard from Germany except the heavy tread of German soldiers' boots at they marched closer to Liege.

On August 4 in Venice, Nancy Johnson received a telegraphed reply from Mr. Laugieri concerning their reservations aboard the *Re d'Italia*. "TWO BERTHS YOUNG LADIES BOOKED ONLY WAY FOR MRS CARROLL WOULD BE TAKE CAPTAINS CABIN THAT HE HAS OFFERED ME FOR REPLY NOT LATER THAN 6 TODAY FOR 1200 FRANCS PLUS 500 FARE[10] NOTWITHSTANDING HIS HAVING BEEN OFFERED ANY PRICE FOR SAME STOP CAPTAINS CABIN HAS TWO PLACES SEE YOUR WAY DIVIDING WIRE REPLY IMMEDIATELY CARE SAVIOTTI GENOVA LAUGIERI"[11]

The sudden price increase for Daisy Carroll's accommodations was more than her husband could afford since he was already spending his own funds to attend to the immediate needs of the Americans who were sleeping on his floors. Nancy made only two reservations for herself and Ethel.

Unbeknownst to Nancy, the transportation situation had hit a roadblock in Genoa. As Arno Behnke noted in his diary: "On Tuesday, August fourth, it was rumored that the *Re d'Italia* would not be able to sail, since the Italian Government had need of it for public uses. On the following day, definite announcement was made at Milan that the *Re d'Italia* would not be able to sail; and that the passengers having been booked by it would have their payments refunded. It was then clear that it was by no means certain that any other ship would be able to sail from an Italian port, and the whole situation was involved in new gloom and uncertainty."[12]

Mr. Laugieri did not know this latest piece of news when he telegraphed Nancy early on August 5: "YOUR BERTHS FIXED LUCKILY FOR YOU POSITION MOST SERIOUS THAUSENDS [sic] AMERICANS HERE CANNOT LEAVE ADVISE YOUR ARRIVAL. LAUGIERI."[13]

By the time Nancy had received this encouraging message, the plans to sail home on the *Re d'Italia* on August 11 had already unraveled. American passengers who had booked the liner's 440 first-class cabins and the larger number of second-class berths were assured that their money would be refunded—though the officials at Navigazione Generale Italiana, the Italian Line, did not specify exactly *when* the refunds would be disbursed. When this chance of escape suddenly evaporated, the Americans, who were scattered among the larger Italian cities, became more panicky. Genoa, the closest Italian seaport to the Atlantic, brimmed over with additional distressed foreigners.

Lack of ready cash was as big a problem as the sudden lack of transportation home. Especially pitiful were the destitute schoolteachers who had literally been pushed out of their hotels when their prepaid time was up. Hotel managers, who were more generous to their wealthy American patrons, acted less kindly toward the middle-class women who worked hard for their daily bread. Now many of the schoolteachers flocked to Genoa to seek help, most of them walking along the roads since they had no money to pay for rail tickets or even to hire a cart.

Louise Vanderbilt saw some of these young women when she and her husband arrived in Genoa, and her warm heart went out to them. "It was pitiful to see so many gently nurtured American women walking about in Genoa's streets in a daze, without any place to sleep," she recalled.[14] Consul General Jones allowed as many of these schoolteachers as possible to sleep on the sofas and chairs of the consulate.

At the Brooklyn Navy Yard, the *Tennessee* prepared to sail. Captain Decker, now back on board his ship, learned the details of his new assignment. The $2.5 million that had been voted by Congress to relieve the distress at American consular offices and embassies in Europe would be shipped aboard the *Tennessee*. All of the money would be in gold. Money from various banks in New York City arrived at the *Tennessee*'s berth under the cloak of darkness on August 4. It took the Marines all night to load the ship's magazine with little oaken casks that were filled to the brim with gold bullion.

The following morning, August 5, anxious relatives flocked to the State and Treasury departments in Washington, D.C., with "little bags of gold" to be sent up to the *Tennessee* for family members in Europe.[15] Among the throng was Congressman Ben Johnson.

"Representative Ben Johnson called at the State Department to-day and left a sum of gold to be cabled,[16] if possible, to his daughter Nancy, who is in Venice. The Department assured the Kentuckian that, if it could not cable the money, it would send it to Miss Johnson aboard the Tennessee. 'We are leaving the matter to Nancy's good judgement,' said Mr. Johnson. 'If it is necessary for her to come home she will come home at once and the money will be available.'"[17]

It was fortunate for all concerned that the volatile Ben Johnson did not know how his daughter's situation in Italy had deteriorated, even as he spoke. While her father was hosting the press, Nancy learned that the *Re d'Italia* would not sail. Furthermore, there appeared to be no other ships scheduled to sail from Italy for America in the foreseeable future. Nor did the congressman's gold ever reach his daughter's hands. The *Tennessee* sailed before Johnson's contribution arrived in New York.[18]

Meanwhile, in Genoa, several prominent New Yorkers had arrived, and they wasted no time bemoaning the Italian government's ban on commercial voyages by ocean liners. They decided to take matters into their own hands.

Well known among his colleagues in New York as the "destroyer of red tape,"[19] RAC Smith concluded that if cabins on an Italian ship could not be procured, then the Americans would charter a ship of their own—or buy it outright if necessary. Consul General Jones, as audacious as Smith, quickly agreed to this novel idea and gave his authorization to proceed under the auspices of the U.S. government, even though Jones had absolutely no authority to do so from U.S. Ambassador Thomas Nelson Page in Rome.

On the morning of August 5, four serious gentlemen repaired to a private room in Genoa's Miramare Hotel, where they drew up a plan of action. Known initially as "the Committee"—and later "the Committee of Guarantors"— these American business titans acted in swift and smooth concert with each other, as if they had been working together all their adult lives. As the docks commissioner of New York's bustling harbor, RAC Smith was unanimously appointed chairman. He would be responsible for the selection and the provisioning of the ship. Known for his linguistic and diplomatic skills, he was in the best position to negotiate terms with the Italian steamship owners. His second in command was Nicholas Butler, fresh off his stolen train from Milan.

The third member of this committee was Gano Dunn, the thirty-three-year-old president of the J. G. White Engineering Corporation. Dunn, who had started out as a telegraph operator at the age of sixteen, worked his way through college, and in 1891 received one of the first degrees conferred in the United States for electrical engineering from Columbia University. As the president of

Frederick W. Vanderbilt, the "silent" member of the Committee of Guarantors, generously donated his personal funds, not only to charter the *Principe di Udine* and pay the surcharge on the coal but also to pay the balance due on the 399 passengers' tickets. Photograph circa 1905. Courtesy of the Shelburne Farms Collections, Shelburne, Vermont

that university, Butler knew that Dunn's abilities would be perfect in the current crisis. The young man once wrote that an engineer was someone who "can do with one dollar what any fool can do with two."[20] With the banks closed and money at a premium, the committee would need every cent Dunn could squeeze.

The fourth member of the committee was a silent partner by his own choice, yet he was also the most important member of the committee. Frederick Vanderbilt's famous name and sterling personal reputation could open doors in Italy that would normally be closed to the others. In short, he was the moneyman, willing and able to buy a ship complete with crew, if necessary. Vanderbilt's legendary wealth awed most of the skittish Italian banking community. While the other three men had been unable to withdraw funds on their letters of credit, Vanderbilt had been permitted to cash ten dollars a day since July 31. With his habitual reticence to seek personal publicity for his charitable works, the shy multimillionaire requested that his pivotal part in this enterprise be kept very quiet. The other three committee members gladly agreed.

At the conclusion of their meeting, Vanderbilt went off to find a bank willing to loan him a fortune in cash. Smith, accompanied by Dunn, set out to search for a likely ship, while Butler and Consul General Jones organized a makeshift ticketing office in the consulate. Smith and Dunn spent the early afternoon of August 5 being rowed around Genoa's "swarming and not overclean" harbor.[21]

One of the many vessels riding at anchor was a two-stack steamer belonging to the Lloyd Sabaudo Line. The *Principe di Udine* was a poky little passenger ship that plied between Genoa and Buenos Aires, taking Italian emigrants to seek work and a new life in Argentina. Launched in 1907, the *Principe di Udine* was exactly 7,828 tons. To the wealthy Americans who were used to traveling aboard huge luxury liners like the *France* at 23,666 tons, or the German behemoth *Imperator* at over 52,000 tons, the *Principe di Udine* looked woefully undersized. On August 5, the ship had been expected to enter dry dock for its annual overhaul and cleaning. Though the *Principe di Udine* was small, slow, and in need of a paint job, it was also available for charter. Smith decided that the *Udine* would do. Once back on shore, he and Butler embarked upon a series of tense negotiations with the ship's owners that turned into a nightmare of greed and bribery over the next few days.

Initially the Lloyd Sabaudo Line agreed to charge the committee 300,000 francs[22] to charter the *Udine* and its crew for a one-way trip to New York, to sail on Wednesday, August 12, without fail. But there was a catch. The steamship company, seeking to kill two birds with one stone and to increase its profits, wanted the *Udine* to call at Palermo and Naples to pick up an additional eleven hundred Italian emigrants who would ride in steerage.

The committee members balked. Smith knew that the staterooms for the first- and second-class passengers were probably smaller than the privileged American travelers were used to. The idea of cramming an additional eleven hundred people into the lowest decks was distasteful and probably unhealthy. Also, stopping at two more ports would delay the ship's eventual crossing by four extra days and could result in ending the *Udine*'s voyage at another Italian port if the government requisitioned the ship for its own use. Smith also realized that his countrymen and women would be anxious to leave Europe altogether and head straight for home. In agreement with Butler, Smith rejected the emigrant proposal. The *Principe di Udine* would be an American ship, chartered with American money for the use of Americans only.

Very well, huffed the officers of the Lloyd Sabaudo Line, in that case the price would have to be higher to offset the lost revenue that the emigrants would have generated. The astronomical sum of 500,000 francs[23] in gold was fixed as the charter price. In his memoirs, Butler wrote that he and Smith "would have signed the contract just the same if 4,000,000 lira had been asked."[24]

The ink was barely dry on the charter contract when RAC Smith and his committee encountered a new series of difficulties. Once the Italians and Americans had agreed upon the final sum, the Lloyd Sabaudo Line began making a number of stipulations. First and foremost was the method of payment. By the terms of the charter, 50,000 francs[25] had to be delivered in gold or hard cash to the Italian steamship officials before 4:30 P.M. on Friday, August 7—less than forty-eight hours away. Furthermore the balance of 450,000 francs[26] had to be paid, again in gold or cash, by Tuesday, August 11, the day before the *Principe di Udine* sailed. No money—no ship.

To raise the necessary funds in such a short time in a country that had placed a moratorium on banking operations was a task of almost insurmountable odds. While the passenger list included a number of millionaires, getting cash-in-hand proved to be a different matter altogether. Back at the consulate, the committee set the rates they would charge their countrymen and women for passage home: $250 for a berth in the ship's first-class accommodations; $100 per person in second class; and $50 for a bunk in the steerage dormitory.[27] The committee members hoped—and prayed—that they could raise the vital down payment from the pockets and purses of their passengers, whom they knew would storm their temporary ticket office the next day. Word of the ship's charter had already spread like a prairie fire through the Americans camped in the various hotels in Genoa.

In the late afternoon of August 5, Nancy Johnson telegraphed the consulate in Genoa, asking if there was another ship on which she and Ethel could obtain passage for home. Instead of Mr. Laugieri, Consul General Jones himself replied: "ADVISE COME TO GENOA TUESDAY[28] WILL RESERVE IF POSSIBLE JONES."[29] At the time of this telegram, Jones did not know if there would be room on board the new ship for Nancy and Ethel. He also suspected that they probably did not have enough money to pay their fare. Nevertheless he felt a strong personal obligation to get these two young Washingtonians home.

After receiving this guarded message that said nothing absolute, Nancy and Ethel sipped their coffee in the pearly twilight above Saint Mark's Square while they pondered their next move. After their experiences getting back from Lausanne, both young women realized that if they lingered any longer in Venice, their opportunities for securing a safe passage back home might decrease from slim to nonexistent in the coming days. On the other hand, the Carrolls had kindly offered them the use of their home for as long as the two

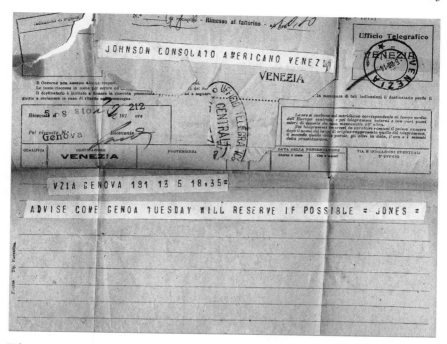

JOHNSON CONSOLATO AMERICANO VENEZIA

VENEZIA

VZIA GENOVA 191 13 5 18,35=

ADVISE COME GENOA TUESDAY WILL RESERVE IF POSSIBLE = JONES =

Telegram sent to Nancy in Venice from U.S. Consul General John Edward Jones in Genoa, August 5, 1914

women wanted to stay. However, the Austrian army was just over the Italian border, not more than a hundred miles away. There was no guarantee that the Austrians would honor Italy's neutrality any more than Germany had honored Belgium's. War news from northern Europe grew more horrifying by the hour.

By twilight on the evening of Wednesday, August 5 in New York City, an additional $5 million was collected from private individuals, many of them family members of the stranded Americans overseas, like Ben Johnson. Some people even delivered their offerings to the *Tennessee* dockside in the Brooklyn Navy Yard.

Col. A. L. Smith of the Quartermaster's Dept. of the army was on board all afternoon, prepared to receive money from anybody who wanted to send help to friends in Europe. About 15 men went on board during the day and gave him sums ranging from $1,000 to $2,000 and, in one case, as high as $5,000.

Benjamin Strong, Jr., President of the Bankers' Trust Company, would not confirm any details of the private gold shipment beyond stating that the amount would be $5,117,000. He said it was planned to establish central stations for relief of stranded Americans in various parts of Europe. The bankers' representatives will buy travelers' checks, drafts and letters of credit at their face value.[30]

On the evening of August 5, the *Tennessee* got under way. The early August 6 edition of the *New York Times* breathlessly reported:

The armored cruiser Tennessee, detailed as a relief ship for the Americans in Europe, left Brooklyn Navy Yard at 7:30 last night and steamed down to the naval anchorage off Thompkinsville, S.I. [Staten Island]. She will leave that place at 10:30 o'clock this morning and sail for Europe, taking with her nearly $8,000,000 in gold.[31] Her exact destination has not been made public. Assistant Secretary of War Breckinridge,[32] who will be in charge of the relief work on the vessel, carries all the orders of the expedition. Mr. Breckenridge arrived in New York last night [August 5], but will not go on board until this morning.

On the Tennessee when she leaves Thompkinsville will be Joseph E. Willard, United States Ambassador to Spain, who is returning to his post from vacation. He will occupy the Admiral's cabin. Mr. Willard did not go on board last night. He is to go down to Thompkinsville this morning.

It was suggested by an amateur naval critic that the ship ought to be painted white instead of her present war color, dull gray, in order to distinguish her at a distance from the vessels of the warring powers, which are all painted about the same color as the Tennessee. There was no time for this, however, and Capt. Decker declared that it was unnecessary.

"When we go up the English Channel," he said, "we'll have her lit up like Luna Park: and in a region where all other ships are trying to make themselves as indistinct as possible they'll have no difficulty in telling who we are."[33]

August 5 had brought more declarations of war. Austria-Hungary formally declared war on Russia and its allies, then France, and now Britain. In turn, Britain and France declared against Turkey, Germany's newest ally. Belgium, shouting a defiant "No!" for the entire world to hear, declared war against Germany, even as the Belgians were fighting a losing battle against that military juggernaut.

The odds against Belgium successfully defending itself were overwhelming. Nearly one-and-a-half-million German soldiers, rank upon rank clad in identical field-gray uniforms, poured over the Belgian and French frontiers.

As they marched in a wide swath through the late summer countryside, the invaders sang "Deutschland über Alles" and "Die Wacht am Rhein."

As the German army drove deeper into Belgium, the USS *Tennessee* cast off from a pier in the Brooklyn Navy Yard and headed down the East River toward the Atlantic on its unique mission of mercy. The *Tennessee* carried not only the gold appropriated by Congress but also additional funds from a number of American financial institutions, including the American Express Company and J. P. Morgan & Company. With little fanfare the cruiser slipped out onto the Atlantic, where it shut down its radio. For the next week or so, the *Tennessee* and its cargo of $8 million in gold virtually disappeared.

Far from the cries of war, another drama was quietly playing out its final act in Washington. In a dimly lit bedroom on the second floor of the White House, President Woodrow Wilson watched throughout the night as his beloved wife slipped quietly away from him.

CHAPTER 10

Gilded Refugees

Ellen Louise Axson Wilson, age fifty-four, died peacefully on August 6, 1914, but for her anguished husband, her passing was the heaviest blow he had ever endured. Kneeling at her bedside, the president sobbed, "Oh, my God! What am I going to do?"[1] The European war was far from his thoughts. Profound grief paralyzed Wilson.

In Genoa, news of the First Lady's death gave little pause among the Americans as they frantically searched for ready cash to cover the first installment for chartering the *Principe di Udine*. In particular, Frederick Vanderbilt felt extremely vulnerable. Never in his privileged life had he experienced a pressing need for money. His personal fortune amounted to over $30 million, yet all he could borrow from a few willing banks in Genoa and Milan was a tiny fraction of the 50,000 francs required by the Lloyd Sabaudo Line. Vanderbilt resented feeling this helpless.

More than once he paused in his search to gaze out at the harbor. If it had not been for the shipwreck incident that he and Louise had suffered in January 1914, their own yacht, the *Warrior,* would have been there in Genoa, ready to take them back to the safety of Hyde Park, New York. Vanderbilt began to entertain second thoughts about his resolution to give up sailing.

At the besieged consulate, John Edward Jones climbed up on a crude platform in the lobby and stared out over the bobbing heads of his anxious countrymen and women. Holding up his hands for silence, he took a deep breath. In ringing tones, he informed the crowd that there *was* a ship, but a small one. The people pressed closer around him. The heat of the Italian August day stifled him; perspiration rolled down the back of his neck. Patiently Jones tried to explain how the steamship tickets could be obtained—even though he himself was not at all sure if their temporary shipping office was going to be able to handle the hundreds of people who surrounded him.

Upstairs, Gano Dunn oversaw the installation of the committee's temporary ticketing office in three vacant rooms. Old tables and wooden chairs had been appropriated as furniture. In one room, several long planks served as a counter. Dunn made sure that there was a wide walkway so that their clients could move easily from one room to the next. Listening to the din below him, Dunn knew that things could turn very ugly if the committee did not maintain tight control of the situation when they opened for business the next day.

On Thursday, August 6, Serbia, in an act of pure defiance against Austria, declared war on Austria's ally, Germany. On Friday, August 5, the tiny country of Montenegro shook off its inertia and declared war on Austria-Hungary. The crimson stain of bloodshed was starting to seep across Europe in a widening pool.

In Belgium, the advancing German army attacked Liege. A Zeppelin L-Z airship, dispatched from Cologne, dropped thirteen bombs on the city, killing nine civilians. In one fell swoop, twentieth-century air warfare was born. Innocent citizens became front line casualties. That night, perhaps for the first time in history, the frightened populace slept in their cellars, seeking protection from the new horror of aerial bombardment.

In Genoa, the deadline for the *Principe di Udine*'s down payment grew closer, and still the Committee of Guarantors had not been able to raise the 50,000–franc down payment for the ship's charter. Butler had only twenty-seven cents in his pocket. Dunn and Smith had very little more between them. In midafternoon of August 7, Vanderbilt again approached the office of the American Express Company, ready to slice off a pound of his own flesh if necessary. This time he spoke directly to Signor Sarentino, the general manager.

The minutes ticked by as one of America's wealthiest men bargained for a loan of cash. Finally, worn down by Vanderbilt's persuasiveness and influenced in no small part by the knowledge of the Vanderbilt fortune in the United States, Signor Sarentino agreed to accept Frederick's personal check for the necessary amount. At 4:25 P.M.—five minutes before the charter contract's option was to have expired—RAC Smith burst through the doors of the Lloyd Sabaudo Line's shipping office with $10,000 in gold. The first hurdle had been cleared.

While Vanderbilt had been squeezing money out of the reluctant bankers, Consul General Jones sent cables to both the State Department and U.S. Ambassador Page in Rome to get their post facto approval for the charter of an Italian ship under the auspices of the U.S. government. Jones knew that he had taken a gamble in agreeing to Smith's plan, but there had been no time to wait for official ratification from his superiors. Page was relieved that Jones had taken the initiative in handling the matter of the distressed Americans, alleviating the American embassy of that burden. Several days later, Washington concurred. By that time, Jones was already hunting for a second ship to charter.

As soon as the first installment had been paid, Smith, Butler, and Dunn met to decide how they were going to choose the fortunate few who would be the *Principe di Udine*'s passengers. Though the little ship could pack over a thousand people in its steerage, the committee realized that the American refugees, many of them traveling with a great deal of baggage, expected much better accommodations. Having surveyed the ship from top to bottom, Smith concluded that it could hold a maximum of four hundred people—the same hallowed number who once danced in Caroline Astor's fabled New York City ballroom. Even that number would be a squeeze—especially for the elite who were not used to being squeezed.

As soon as the *Udine*'s charter was assured on August 7, Jones sent a hurried telegram to Nancy Johnson in Venice, who was chewing her fingernails with indecision. The Carrolls had told Nancy and Ethel that no one could sail from Genoa. Coal supplies were dwindling. It would be more prudent for the two women to remain with them in Venice.

Jones's message came right to the point: "TO NANCY JOHNSON CONSOLATO AMERICANO VENEZIA—COME I WILL SEE YOU THROUGH JONES."[2]

To keep this promise, Jones also sent ever-smiling and reassuring Mr. Laugieri back to Venice to escort Nancy and Ethel to Genoa. If Nancy continued to dither, Jones vowed that he would personally push the hesitant young woman up the *Udine*'s gangplank next Wednesday morning. He did not want the powerful Congressman Ben Johnson howling for his head on a platter.

Early on Sunday, August 9, Nancy and Ethel bade good-bye to the Carrolls for a second time. Accompanied once again by their mountain of luggage and Mr. Laugieri, the women boarded the westbound train to Milan. They anticipated a pleasant day trip to Genoa. But a lot had happened to railway schedules in the week since Nancy had spent the night in Switzerland. Because of the increasing coal shortages, their train arrived late in Milan, stopping at every station along the route. Instead of reaching Genoa in the late afternoon as they had expected, Nancy and Ethel sat up all night in a stifling, crowded day coach. They kept each other awake, fearing that someone might steal their luggage if they slept. When they finally arrived in Genoa on Monday morning, August 10, with red-rimmed eyes and frayed nerves, they were in for yet another nasty surprise. The streets of Genoa seethed with mobs of frightened Americans.

Though Venice had experienced its share of frantic American tourists arriving at Carroll's office, the horrors of war itself seemed very remote. Genoa presented a completely different picture. The weary women were stunned to see many Americans wandering the streets near the consulate in travel-stained disheveled clothing, with disarrayed hair, and with few personal belongings. Everyone's face bore a certain pinched look about the eyes and lips. A shocking number of people, obviously well-bred, were actually begging for money on the street corners. The sight appalled Nancy. For the first time, she fully grasped the dire predicament that she was in. But for the grace of God and the personal protection of several U.S. officials, she, too, could have been out begging on the filthy streets of Genoa.

By the time Mr. Laugieri and the two women arrived at the consulate on the early morning of August 10, Jones's energies had begun to flag from lack of sleep, although he was certainly glad to see that Nancy and Ethel had made it through safely. He dashed off a cable to the State Department: "NOTIFY REPRESENTATIVE BEN JOHNSON NANCY AND ETHEL IN MY CARE GENOA SAILING WEDNESDAY JONES"[3]

Later that day, across the Atlantic in Washington, Johnson received the consul general's message while attending a meeting of the congressional Committee on the District of Columbia. He immediately called his wife with the good news. Annie Johnson passed the message on to Ethel's mother. Typically Johnson also called a press conference later that afternoon. He was in good spirits, and he wanted the world to know it.

> Information was received in Washington yesterday [August 11] that Miss Nancy Johnson, daughter of Representative and Mrs. Ben Johnson of Kentucky, would sail today from Genoa, Italy, on the steamer Udine. This bit of comforting news to Miss Johnson's friends and relatives was contained in a cablegram from John Edwards Jones, United States consul general at Genoa, under whose care Miss Johnson placed herself when it became evident that hostilities would break out between the great nations of Europe.
>
> Friends Anxious About Her. Much anxiety was felt here when Austria declared war against Serbia. Miss Johnson was then visiting Dr. and Mrs. Carroll in Venice. These fears were somewhat allayed when it became known some days later that she had reached Genoa safely, and that she was being cared for at the American consulate.[4]

Nancy and Ethel were not the only stray Americans who were seeking transportation at the Genoa consulate. Since the Committee of Guarantors' ad hoc ticket office had opened for business on Saturday, the building had been the scene of bedlam. By Monday morning, August 10, the committee, under Gano Dunn's direction, had smoothed out the berth assignments and payment procedure for the *Principe di Udine* into a model of calm efficiency.

People who had registered at the consulate during the past week, as well as newer arrivals in Genoa, were directed to the first table staffed by a committee volunteer, Henry Haskell of New York City. Haskell had the unenviable job of listening to hours of woeful tales describing lost baggage, closed banks, and rude accommodations. He, in turn, gave out the pertinent information about the chartered ship, such as the date and time of its sailing and the ticket prices.

Sitting at the next desk, Smith and Butler sorted out the remaining available stateroom assignments, and they juggled the delicate problem of cabinmates. The ship was far too small and the demand too high to permit everyone to have private cabins. If the prospective passengers were still interested in sailing on the *Principe di Udine,* they were sent to the next table where another volunteer, Louis Ray, headmaster of the Irving School in New York City, recorded their names and their addresses both in the United States and in Genoa. Stationed beside Ray was James Lewis, another New Yorker, who was responsible for preparing the official passenger list for the ship's manifest.

Having completed the reservation process, the passengers went into the adjoining room, where Gano Dunn, acting as the committee's treasurer, received them. Most of the Americans became very sheepish at this point when they had to confess their embarrassing lack of funds. Though Nancy and Ethel had started out for Paris on July 31 with uncashed checks for $100 apiece, by the time they presented themselves before Dunn, they had only a few dollars and change between them. The cost of train tickets and other services had skyrocketed over the past ten days.

Despite her shortage of funds, Nancy insisted on purchasing a first-class berth at $250. She assured the smiling young man behind the desk that her father was wiring sufficient money to pay for her passage. Dunn was well aware of the continuing problem with cabled funds; nevertheless, he accepted Nancy's and Ethel's letters of credit for the balance due. No doubt Jones had told Dunn that Nancy carried a letter of introduction from President Wilson, or perhaps the personable bachelor was merely following the rule of thumb that preference should be given to women traveling alone or to those with children. From Saturday, August 8, through Tuesday, August 11, Dunn amassed a large collection of currency: francs, lire, dollars, personal checks, American Express notes, letters of credit, and one IOU. All totaled, the sum came to a little less than $60,000[5] in ready cash. Unbeknownst to the desperate Americans who could not scrape up the full amount for their passage, Frederick Vanderbilt's quiet generosity had covered the $40,000 deficit.

Postcard of the SS *Principe di Udine*–the "Refugee Ship."

Helping Dunn to sort through the confusing pile of loose change and notes were George Stearns, a prominent textile manufacturer from Augusta, Georgia, and Dr. W. O. Bartlett, of Boston. When the financial arrangements had been concluded to the satisfaction of Dunn, Stearns, and Bartlett, the anxious passenger then passed along to the final table where an agent from the Lloyd Sabaudo Line issued the precious steamship tickets. All of these gentlemen worked long hours, especially late Monday and Tuesday (August 10 and 11) nights, in the effort to cram as many of their compatriots—and their inevitable mountains of baggage—into the *Principe di Udine* as comfortably as possible. The final passenger list numbered 399 refugees. Not on the passenger list, but pictured in Arno Behnke's book, *The Sailing of the Refugee Ship*, was the four hundredth passenger: a half-grown black kitten that had probably been picked up out of a Genoa gutter by one of the *Udine*'s tender-hearted young women. The cat had no listed name on the passenger manifest, but he was designated as "the mascot" by Behnke.[6]

Six decades later, Nancy Johnson Crawford chuckled when she thought of herself as a "refugee." "What a pack we were!" she remarked as she reminisced in the living room of her sunny apartment in Alexandria, Virginia.[7] Never before had the immigrant ship *Principe di Udine* carried such illustrious passengers.

Though Frederick and Louise Vanderbilt were certainly the wealthiest and most prominent couple on board, they had excellent company: the president of the New York State Railway; a noted urological surgeon from Mount Sinai Hospital; the retired medical director of the U.S. Navy; a New York book publisher; a founder of the Standard Oil Company; an official of the U.S. Patent Office; the former mayor of New York City; and the editor in chief of the *Washington Star*.[8]

In addition there were ten other doctors: medical, academic, and divinity; two judges; one college president; three professors; five reverend ministers; two bishops; several heads of companies; one colonel in the U.S. Army; a number of lawyers—and one congressman's daughter. Twenty-seven families shepherded sixty children between the ages of ten and thirty. The largest group of all were the ninety-eight unaccompanied, single women, including Nancy and Ethel.

These gilded refugees represented thirty-eight states, the District of Columbia, and Puerto Rico. The majority claimed New York City and environs as home, but others came from such far-flung places as Sheboygan Falls, Wisconsin; Grand Rapids, Michigan; Middleton, Ohio; Oklahoma City, Oklahoma; Canton, Missouri; San Antonio, Texas; and Los Angeles. A total of 166 men and 233 women were scheduled to sail aboard the *Principe di Udine* on Wednesday, August 12, at noon.[9]

On Sunday, August 9, the first of eighty thousand troops of the British Expeditionary Force embarked from Southampton and Portsmouth for Belgium. On Monday, August 10, France finally declared war on Austria-Hungary.

And far out in the middle of the Atlantic Ocean, the USS *Tennessee* plowed deep furrows through the waves toward England. It was bringing golden relief.

No sooner had the down payment for the *Principe di Udine* been met than the members of the Committee of Guarantors had to face their next hurdle: collecting the balance. It was readily apparent that the passengers themselves did not have sufficient cash to cover the cost of the ship's charter price. Once again, Smith and Vanderbilt set off in search of funds. The final payment of 450,000 francs was due by noon on Tuesday, August 11—a scant three-and-a-half days away.

To compound the problem, the onset of war had inflated the market price of gold by 15 percent. Also, the service charges of the American Express Company and the Italian banks that had accepted Vanderbilt's letters of credit now increased the required sum by an additional 75,000 francs.[10] On top of these extra costs, the Lloyd Sabaudo Line told the committee members that Italian military requirements had made coal for civilian use extremely difficult to obtain. With crocodilian regret, the steamship company added a surcharge of 90 francs[11] a ton for the coal necessary to sail the ship to New York. RAC Smith could only gnash his teeth.[12]

Consul General Jones sent more urgent wires to the State Department, pleading for money. In reply he was told that the department had in fact cabled two hundred thousand dollars to the U.S. ambassador in London, Walter Page, on August 5, with instructions to send one hundred thousand dollars to Ambassador Myron Herrick in Paris and twenty-five thousand dollars to Ambassador Thomas Page in Italy. When Jones wired his superior in Rome, Page told him that he had received nothing from London. London's Ambassador Page snapped back that the State Department's cable had been held up by the British censor. London's Page could not send nonexistent funds to Rome's Page.[13]

Meanwhile Smith discovered that the National City Bank of New York had a very large cash deposit sitting in the vaults of several banks in Genoa. Smith, Vanderbilt, and Dunn immediately wired their banks in New York, asking them to transfer funds from their personal accounts to the National City Bank. National, in turn, could then directly cable the Genoa banks with instructions to deliver the necessary money to the Americans. The plan, on paper, was an excellent one, but once again the cables to and from New York were delayed or lost because of the escalating war frenzy.

RAC Smith sent an urgent personal plea to his friend Frank Vanderlip, the president of the National City Bank, on Sunday, August 9. Incredibly this cable got through to New York without holdup. Vanderlip responded immediately. He wired Genoa via London to transfer the money that Smith so urgently needed. In addition, Vanderlip sent a personal cable to the president of the Banca Commerciale in Genoa that the funds had indeed been transferred at his behest and to honor Smith's request immediately.

On Monday morning, with less than forty-eight hours until the *Principe di Udine* was due to sail, the Italian bank president turned skittish. He told Smith that he could not release over five hundred thousand francs on the mere evidence of Vanderlip's telegram. He needed additional confirmation from the Bank of England in London that the money was indeed there. Again, owing to the long delays and the rigid censorship among the belligerents, the necessary cables did not go through.

Miraculously, on Monday afternoon, August 10, Signor Sarentino, general manager of the American Express office in Genoa, again came to the committee's rescue. Once more, he agreed to accept Smith's, Dunn's, and Vanderbilt's personal checks and written guarantees for the balance of payment to the Lloyd Sabaudo Line.[14] In addition, at Vanderbilt's suggestion, the committee drew additional funds, which they presented to Jones for the neediest Americans on his doorstep. The continuing plight of the destitute schoolteachers had particularly moved Vanderbilt to set up this emergency fund.[15] At the end of the day, Smith and his committee were satisfied with the arrangements. Butler thought that it was "money well spent."[16]

In Washington the members of Congress, overwhelmed with telegrams and telephone calls from their constituents who had family and friends abroad, authorized the sailing of a second "treasure ship." The armored cruiser USS *North Carolina*, sister ship of the USS *Tennessee*, left its berth in the Boston Navy Yard on Saturday, August 8, with an undisclosed sum locked in its ammunition magazine. The *North Carolina* had orders to proceed to England, where it would join the *Tennessee*. From Falmouth, the two American warships would then sail to other European ports, bringing monetary relief for U.S. citizens.

While John Edward Jones was glad to learn that help was literally on the way, he needed funds immediately. The windfall of Vanderbilt's unselfish generosity, especially at a time when almost everyone's thoughts were for personal comfort and escape from the war, nearly moved the overworked consul general to tears. By the second week of August, there were nearly five thousand Americans stranded in Genoa. Some of them were burdened with children crying to go home. Others had no money at all to pay for their most basic needs. All of them sought immediate escape from the escalating warfare.[17]

On Wednesday, August 12, Great Britain finally declared war on Austria-Hungary. In Belgium, the huge German siege guns drew closer to Liege.

Meanwhile, in Genoa, Wednesday, August 12, dawned sunny and hot. It seemed as if the entire city had converged upon the harbor to witness the first chartered ship depart for the safe shores of the United States. Although Jones had been awake almost round the clock since early Monday morning, today he felt buoyant, ready to celebrate the culmination of a week filled with financial worries, hysterical people, and monumental red tape. Despite his fatigue, he dressed jauntily for the occasion in patriotic colors: a blue blazer, white flannel trousers, and a red rose in his buttonhole. The last thing he expected this morning was yet another crisis literally under his own roof.

In the front hall of the consul's house where they had been staying as Jones's guests, Nancy and Ethel waited for transportation to the wharf, surrounded by their numerous cases and trunks. When Jones saw the pile of baggage, he suggested that the young women pick one or two of the most necessary pieces and leave the rest. He had inspected the interior of the *Principe di Udine* on several occasions, and he knew that space was going to be very tight.

Nancy shook her head. She had come to Italy with twenty-six pieces of luggage, hauled every bit of it around with her for the past two weeks, and would return home in the same fashion, with every bag accounted for. Her father would expect nothing less from her. Ben Johnson had always insisted that his children be very careful of their belongings.

Jones groaned under his breath. In firmer tones, he told Nancy to choose what she needed and that he would send the rest when it was possible.

In answer, Nancy sat down on top of the nearest wardrobe trunk and tapped the tip of her parasol on the marble floor for emphasis. She would not leave until all her baggage accompanied her. No doubt Jones momentarily entertained the idea of taking Nancy at her word and giving her berth to someone else—perhaps to another one of those destitute schoolteachers. But then he realized that if the congressman's stubborn daughter stayed in Genoa, she—and her blasted suitcases—would be literally underfoot in his home. Not to mention what hell would be paid to Jones's future career in the State Department if the "president's personal friend" did not arrive in New York on time as promised.

Nancy allowed a few tears to roll down her cheeks. Swallowing his exasperation, the exhausted consul general called for a cart to convey Nancy's and Ethel's personal effects. Then he helped the two women into his car, and they sped to the wharf, where the *Principe di Udine* awaited its glittering passengers.

Decades later, Nancy's grandchildren expressed surprise at her adamant refusal to abandon her baggage as so many other Americans had done that August. Nancy agreed that the incident indeed sounded silly in retrospect, but "it seemed very important to me at the time."[18]

The wide promenade on the wharf seethed with a mass of people, both Italians and Americans. Nancy, who had always felt claustrophobic in the midst of large crowds, was appalled when their car stopped at the head of the bustling pier. Baggage porters, sweating under their loads of heavy trunks and suitcases, struggled up and down the single gangplank into the *Udine*. Dodging these workers, the passengers bumped against one another in their efforts to board quickly—as if they were afraid the little steamship would sail away without them.

Arno Behnke described the scene at the quayside: "Probably no one of the refugees will ever forget the scene at the Genoa wharf as the time for departure drew near. . . . Vendors of gaudy steamer chairs competed with the peddlers of cheap binoculars to get the last few *centissimi* from the slim purses of the departing voyagers. The poor, disappointed Americans, who had to stay behind, tried to be cheerful and to wish us enthusiastic 'God-speeds' while the never-to-be-forgotten Italian band struggled heroically to render the *Star Spangled Banner* with enthusiasm and éclat."[19]

U.S. Consul General John Edward Jones bids good-bye to the Americans aboard the *Principe di Udine* before they sail from Genoa, August 12, 1914. Photograph from *The Sailing of a Refugee Ship*

Gripped by the urgency that rippled through the sultry morning air, Nancy clutched her handbag, parasol, and overnight case. "With a companion, Miss Norris, she pushed her way on ship as thousands begged piteously for passage."[20]

Up on the bridge, Consul General Jones shook hands with the beaming members of the Committee of Guarantors for the last time. Captain Tiscornia, master of the *Principe di Udine,* warned Jones that departure was imminent. Another round of handshakes, then the consul general walked down the gangplank. Midway he paused, turned back to look at all the people he had helped, and waved farewell. With their grateful applause ringing in his ears, he stepped ashore.

When the final passenger literally ran up the gangway of the crowded vessel, the *Udine* took in its lines and began to move away from the pier. The lucky passengers lined the railings, waving little American flags that someone from the consulate had given them. The *Udine* blew its whistle. The tugs dropped behind in its frothy wake, and very quickly the city of Genoa receded from view. The voyage toward home and safety began in earnest. The sense of relief among the passengers aboard the ship was palpable.

Arno Behnke observed in his memoir of the voyage that "probably very few genuine refugees crossing the Atlantic have ever enjoyed all the privileges of a private yacht, as everyone on the *Principe* did."[21]

The Dartmouth sophomore quickly realized that history was being made even as the ship was leaving Genoa's ancient harbor. During the next two weeks of the *Principe di Udine*'s voyage to New York, this enterprising young man interviewed the passengers, took notes, and found kindred spirits in Fred White of New York City, who took a number of photographs of the ship's departure as well as candids taken on board, and Rose Churchill of New Britain, Connecticut, who rendered a few sketches of the trip. Another fellow passenger, Gustave Schirmer, who was a book publisher in New York, kindly offered the services of his press. Together the three young people and the sympathetic book publisher created a permanent record of their escape from Europe and the journey home.

Once the *Principe di Udine* had left Genoa, Consul General Jones cabled Nancy's anxious parents in Washington, D.C., that Nancy and Ethel were on their way home. Ever ready to reap good publicity, Ben Johnson alerted the

Passengers wave final farewells from the rail of the *Principe di Udine* as it leaves the dock in Genoa, August 12, 1914. Photograph from *The Sailing of a Refugee Ship*

press in both Washington and Kentucky that his daughter would soon be back in the United States.

"She Will Quit Genoa," wrote the *Washington Post* on August 12.

Miss Nancy Johnson to Leave Today for America. Friends' Anxiety Allayed. Daughter of Representative and Mrs. Ben Johnson Was in Venice When Hostilities Between Austria and Servia [*sic*] Broke Out—Afterward Put Herself Under Protection of American Consul.

Information was received in Washington yesterday that Miss Nancy Johnson of Kentucky, would sail today from Genoa, Italy, on the steamer Udine. This bit of comforting news to Miss Johnson's friends and relatives was contained in a cablegram from John Edward Jones, United States consul general at Genoa, under whose care Miss Johnson placed herself when it became evident that hostilities would break out between the great nations of Europe.

Friends Anxious About Her. Much anxiety was felt here for Miss Johnson's safety when Austria declared war against Servia. Miss Johnson was then visiting Dr. and Mrs. Carroll in Venice. These fears were somewhat allayed when it became known some days later that she had reached Genoa safely, and that she was being cared for at the American consulate.[22]

"During the first few days out, the experiences undergone on the Continent formed the principle [*sic*] topic for conversation with young and old alike. The more harrowing adventures went the rounds of the ship with amazing rapidity," Behnke began his narrative of the *Udine*'s journey.[23]

To accommodate everyone during mealtimes in the manner to which the Americans were accustomed, two sittings for luncheon and dinner were set up in both the *Udine*'s first-class and second-class dining rooms. The ship's waiters and stewards were perpetually in motion from early morning until after eleven o'clock at night, attending to the wants and needs of their privileged clientele.

That evening, during their first dinner at sea, Nancy and Ethel heard some of their tablemates' stories of the experiences that they had endured in their escapes across Europe to Genoa. The tales ran the gamut from the sublime to the ridiculous.

"We had just ended a motor trip at San Sebastian, Spain when the war broke out," Dr. Virgil Parker of Brooklyn began. "On Saturday, August 1st, we boarded a train for Marseilles in order to make our boat back to America the following Monday. In San Sebastian, we knew nothing whatsoever about the war between France and Germany. Only after we passed the French border and seen [sic] soldiers guarding the tracks and the fields destitute of men, did we surmise that something unusual was going on."[24]

"At one place, the French soldiers had barricaded the road with logs and in two other places with chains. We got through without difficulty every time we were stopped," E. T. Holmes, president of the Holmes Electric Protective Company, remarked with a twinkle in his eyes. "Our little French maid exchanged a few jovial words with the guards."[25]

Louis Ray concurred with his own story of the ineptitude of the Austrian border police. "We started our motor trip up the wonderful mountains above Trieste. Halfway up, a soldier stopped us and demanded our travel permit. This he 'read' upside down, pronounced good, and then allowed us to pass."[26] Laughter ran round the table at this story. It felt good to laugh again.

"The tragedy of it all came upon me in one brief second," Edwin Thanhouser told his listeners. "One morning early, I stood at my bedroom window in Argentiere watching a troop train pull out. The recruits shouted the 'Marseillaise' with tremendous enthusiasm. Then suddenly, while their shouting still echoed in the distance, I heard a great wail below me and looking down, I saw the mother and sister of one of those boys sobbing as if their hearts would break. Never before have I experienced such a dramatic effect—first the song and then the sob. It was tragic."[27] Thanhouser knew a dramatic moment when he saw it. He had been an actor in the 1880s and was now a motion picture producer.[28]

Professor William Newbold, who taught at the University of Pennsylvania, nodded his head. "When we finally reached the streets of Munich, we found them full of singing soldiers. *Die Wacht am Rhein* and *Deutschland Uber Alles* rang out from thousands of patriotic throats. It was thrilling, but it also sent shivers down my spine to hear that fervor to kill fellow beings."[29]

By silent but mutual consent, the dinner table talk turned to lighter topics. But the war did not go away. Even as the passengers finished their desserts and sipped their after-dinner coffees under the Mediterranean's starry sky, the conflict in Belgium increased its terrifying devastation. The German siege guns had finally arrived outside of Liege. It took a team of thirty-six horses to drag one of the cannons down the dusty roads. At 6:30 P.M. on August 12, the Germans fired the initial shot at Fort Pontisse, one of the defensive fortifications that ringed Liege and had, until now, repulsed the previous German efforts to take the city.

During the next few days, other stories of privations and sufferings circulated around the ship. While chatting on deck with her fellow passengers, Nancy heard more chilling episodes.

"When we left our hotel at Karer See, only four guests remained in an establishment which was built to accommodate 450."

"We saw the devastation of war all about us."

"I saw the strained faces of the men and the tear-wet faces of the women."

"Our only meal that night consisted of a few rolls left over from luncheon and a bottle of water."

"With the shifting of the wind, we smelled alternately the pungent smoke of battle or the earthly fragrance of newly harvested fields."

"Marseilles fairly shook with the tramp of marching feet."

"I had $4300.00 in American Express travelers' checks and 3 francs in cash."

"People had to sleep in the parks and streets."

"The scene at the Munich Station baffles description. We became jammed between piles of baggage fifteen feet high."[1]

Nancy added her own observation of what she had witnessed in Genoa. "I saw a man with $100,000[2] in good paper money beg for something to eat," she recalled with a shudder.[3]

As the first few tranquil days at sea passed by with calm seas and warm evenings, the homeward-bound Americans slowly turned their thoughts away from the war they had left behind them. Instead, the passengers dozed in deck chairs, read books, and mulled over the dilemma of "what shall we do to pass the time between luncheon and dinner?"

Fortunately, the Committee on Entertainments had been formed within the first twenty-four hours of the voyage. This energetic group of passengers

quickly arranged for dances and deck sports for the large crowd of young people who were on board. For the older or more intellectual sort, the committee
planned a series of lectures, which were given every afternoon following lunch.
Some of the topics were of general interest, such as RAC Smith's "The Ship
That Sailed," during which he explained how the *Principe di Udine* had been
chartered. Others were more erudite, such as Paul S. Reinsch, U.S. minister to
China, who gave a talk on "American Business Work in China."

Nancy, who loved to play cards, spent many afternoons playing bridge with
like-minded souls.

On the evening of August 15, around 7:30 P.M., the *Principe di Udine* passed
Gibraltar heading toward the Atlantic. Nancy was again on deck as she had
been nearly two months earlier when she had passed "The Rock" on the way
to Italy. At that time, she had been thrilled to see Africa on one side and Europe
on the other. This time there was a different exciting experience.

"Our first contact with the war after we left Genoa happened at Gibraltar,
the third evening out," Behnke wrote in his "Unofficial Log" of the trip.

> The sun had just gone down behind the historic rock, and the soft dark-
> ness of twilight was beginning to cast a haze over its sharp outlines when
> all of a sudden, a small torpedo boat destroyer speeded towards us from
> the shadows. Since Dr. Butler had prepared for such an incident before
> weighing anchor by obtaining permission through the kindness of Win-
> ston Churchill, First Lord of the [British] Admiralty, to pass Gibraltar, and
> since the American flag was at the peak, we felt pretty sure that we would
> not be delayed. Yet it caused a thrill to see the little belligerent vessel ap-
> proach with the swiftness of a greyhound. When it came alongside, one of
> the Englishmen flashed the white beam of a powerful searchlight first at
> our colors and then at our decks crowded with passengers who had turned
> out to see the King's fighting ship.
>
> The English officer in command called the customary, "Where are you
> from and where are you bound?" and upon receiving the reply, "From
> Genoa to New York, carrying American citizens," he ordered the inquisi-
> tive ray turned off, and then, with a final "Thank you," directed his little
> craft back to the protecting rock. A lusty cheer from four hundred Ameri-
> can throats followed his vessel across the water.[4]

Before the torpedo boat returned to its base, Committee of Guarantors
member Gano Dunn, who spent a great deal of time in the *Principe di Udine*'s
wireless shack, sent a partial passenger list to the British base on Gibraltar. The
British, in turn, wired the list to Cadiz, Spain. In turn, Cadiz wired the list to

New York, where it was published the following day in the *New York Times*. Unfortunately some of the names were garbled during the multiple transmissions. Not only was Nancy Johnson listed as a passenger, but so was her father, "Congressman Ben Johnson." Likewise Ethel Norris was listed with a slight modification. She was supposed to be traveling with her father, "Senator" Norris. Ethel's father was a lawyer for the Justice Department.[5]

Dunn, whose background and expertise were in electrical engineering, enjoyed "listening" in on the *Principe di Udine*'s wireless set at various times during the day to keep abreast of the world news. Each morning and evening, Dunn posted news bulletins in the ship's saloon. Nighttime wireless messages tended to be clearer and had a longer range. During the early part of the trip, Dunn's bulletins contained news of German victories as the kaiser's war machine mowed across Belgium.

On Sunday, August 16, while divine services were being conducted aboard the *Principe di Udine,* the gold ship USS *Tennessee* steamed into Falmouth, England, with all its flags and bunting flying. The ship's trip had been uneventful. It had met one British cruiser and a French cruiser, but never sighted one of the dreaded German submarines. Upon docking, Assistant Secretary of War Henry Breckinridge, who had accompanied the treasure across the ocean, and his minions departed immediately for London. Meanwhile the unloading of the precious cargo was delayed until the following day, so that Lloyds of London, the maritime insurance company, could legally cover the tricky transfer of over $4 million in gold from ship to small boat to shore.

Captain Decker, relaxed and cheerful now that he had crossed the Atlantic safely, jauntily told the British officials, "Take it when you like. It is all safe and sound. All I want is your autograph when you receive it."[6]

Early in the morning of August 17, once the responsibility for the gold was transferred to Lloyds, the heavy little kegs were wrapped securely in a sail, and then dropped by a large derrick into a waiting sailing vessel. The boat, now low in the water from the weight of the treasure, was then towed to a nearby wharf. The entire operation was watched closely by a large number of local residents from Falmouth.

After the kegs made it safely ashore, the Marines loaded them on a wagon, and they were taken to a special steel bullion railway car. The gold train left Falmouth around 11:30 A.M., and upon arrival in London, the money was deposited in the vaults at the Bank of England on Threadneedle Street.

Ambassador Walter Page, who warmly welcomed the *Tennessee*'s gold, immediately transferred $300,000 to Herbert Hoover's beleaguered American Citizen's Relief Committee. The rest of the *Tennessee*'s gleaming cargo was destined for the American consulate in Rotterdam.[7] The following day, the second gold cruiser sent by Congress, the USS *North Carolina*, joined its sister ship in Falmouth harbor.

Almost buried amid the fast-breaking news of the war was the notice that Pope Pius X had taken ill and had gone to bed. The first report, issued by the Vatican on August 16, stated, "Pope Pius is ill mentally as well as physically. The war has been the greatest shock the Pontiff has ever had, coming when he is enfeebled by age and by the intense heat of a Roman summer. He is suffering from a gouty catarrh, with a rise in temperature, and has been ordered to bed by his physician."[8]

While this saintly man lay ailing in Rome, the butchery in Europe began in earnest, especially in Belgium. Despite a gallant defense, Liege finally fell under the onslaught of the massive German siege guns on August 17. The victors poured through the rubble of the forts that had surrounded the city. Many innocent civilians were shot in reprisal for defending their homes and towns. Entire villages were burned to the ground as the German army swept through the countryside.

The cries of war drifted far behind the *Principe di Udine* as it headed across the Atlantic. The sight of the emerald green Azores brought many people out on deck as the ship passed by them. And early risers, like Nancy, enjoyed watching the amazing flying fish that leaped along the sides of the ship in the predawn hours. These sights did much to cheer the passengers and helped them to forget, at least for a little while, the frightening experiences they had all endured.

On Tuesday, August 18, at 10:30 A.M., the *Principe di Udine* crossed the halfway point in its journey. The Committee of Guarantors arranged a little ceremony on deck to encourage the passengers. While the vessel's Italian master, Captain Tiscornia, and committee members Smith, Butler, and Dunn stood on the bridge, the American flag was hoisted to the forepeak. Amid cheers, and some tears of joy, the ship's whistle saluted the Stars and Stripes. Frederick Vanderbilt, the fourth man who should have been on the bridge with the other members of the committee, preferred to keep his own part in the venture in low profile. Perhaps he did not want to make the passengers feel uncomfortable to see the man to whom they all owed a good deal of money— as well as their passage on board the ship.

Later that day, the ship's passengers enjoyed a delicious luncheon and the afternoon's lecture, "Italy's Relation to the Present War," presented by George B. McClellan Jr., son of the famous Civil War general and himself a former mayor of New York City. Following McClellan's remarks, the passengers were

Three members of the Committee of Guarantors and Captain Tiscornia, the master of the *Principe di Udine,* pose on the ship's bridge during the midcrossing celebration on August 18, 1914 (L to R): Gano Dunn, Captain Tiscornia, RAC Smith, and Dr. Nicholas Butler. Photograph from *The Sailing of a Refugee Ship*

asked to remain in the saloon. Under the guidance of Nicholas Butler and with more applause, they passed a resolution that praised Consul General Jones and the work he had done to secure their passage aboard the *Principe di Udine.* "We desire to recognize the sympathy and kindness with which the Consul General, ably seconded by his office force, treated each one of us, making our troubles his own, cheering us up when we were losing heart, and seeking out special cases of need among our afflicted countrymen and women."[9]

Nancy was at this meeting, and she agreed wholeheartedly that Jones, indeed, was "the right man, in the right place, at the right time." When the passengers voted the resolution to "publish to our country the unwearied faithfulness of our Consul General in acting day and night for our relief," Nancy enthusiastically added her voice. It was a promise that she would keep before the month was out.[10]

After midnight, in the early morning hours of August 19, Gano Dunn visited the wireless shack where he heard amid the "confused rattle of clickings and tappings" that Pope Pius X had become gravely ill. The day before, Dunn had learned that the pope was bed-ridden with gout, but now, it appeared, his illness was much worse than anyone had suspected. As the hours wore on until dawn, the news from Rome continued to sound more dire. Dunn posted a guarded message, reporting only that the pope was failing.

Nancy was deeply troubled when she read this message on her way through the saloon to breakfast. Perhaps a little twinge of conscience nagged her. She could have met him only a month ago.

Throughout the day Dunn haunted the wireless shack, waiting for more news. The spirits aboard the ship were more subdued on the 19th, even though many of the passengers were non-Catholic. Religion aside, the pope was a world leader and the most powerful voice for peace that had been heard during the past three weeks of tension and warmongering.

At 1:20 in the early morning of August 20, Pope Pius X died in the Vatican at Rome. According to one of the cardinals who attended the pope's final hours, Pius said, "Now I begin to think, as the end is approaching, that the Almighty, in His inexhaustible goodness, wishes to spare me the horrors Europe is undergoing."[11]

Gano Dunn continued to monitor further messages on the wireless to confirm this report. By midmorning of August 20, there was no doubt. The pope was dead. Dunn made a black-bordered announcement card and wrote, "It is officially announced that His Holiness, Pope Pius the Tenth has died."[12]

As a practicing Catholic who took her religion seriously, Nancy was deeply shocked and saddened. Reacting to the situation with her usual horror of death, she retired to her cabin to pray for the pope's soul since there was no chapel on board the ship. She remained there the rest of the day.[13]

At five o'clock the following afternoon, August 21, the *Principe di Udine*'s wireless suddenly crackled with a direct order from an unseen ship following behind them. This latest news caused a stir of panic throughout the passengers and crew alike. They were just seven hundred miles from New York and the safety of home. The decks filled with passengers, anxious to see who was chasing them. Nancy was among them, as was Arno Behnke, who jotted down the events as they happened:

> "To I.Y.U.," it called. [I.Y.U. is the wireless name for the *Principe di Udine*] "Stop your ship by order of our commander. Tell your captain to stop his engines and await us."
>
> Our operator, Signor Amici, asked "Please give your name."
>
> "We are an English warship," was the reply.

The passengers aboard the *Principe di Udine* watch the British warship sail
past them, August 21, 1914. Photograph from *The Sailing of a Refugee Ship*

Then Signor Amici answered for Captain Tiscornia, "Your message received. Our engines are stopped."

The other continued, "To I.Y.U.: Please tell us from what port you
sailed, where are you bound, what cargo you have, and how many passengers."

We replied, "To English warship: From Genoa to New York. Little general merchandise. 399 passengers, American citizens. Vessel chartered by
American Consul General."

Then came the response, "You may proceed. Sorry to have delayed you.
Wish you pleasant voyage."[14]

The English warship was the HMS *Caronia*, a British ocean liner recently
commandeered by the Royal Navy and outfitted with deck guns as an armed
merchant cruiser. It was commissioned into the Royal Navy on August 8,
1914. It was no wonder that its commanding officer sounded skittish with the
Principe di Udine. He had been in a wartime command for less than two
weeks.[15]

Behnke continued:

While this conversation was going on, the black hull and smoking funnels grew larger and larger as the vessel approached us, churning white
foam in the indigo sea. When the ship drew near, the excitement on the
Udine became intense; passengers crowded even high up on the life-boats
in order to get an unobstructed view of His majesty's man-o-war. Our vessel, with flags flying from every mast and with hundreds of passengers lin-
ing the rails, must have presented a brilliant spectacle to the Britishers [*sic*];
and certainly, the auxiliary cruiser made an interesting sight to us as she
steamed past. With binoculars, we could make out her formidable guns,
and even the red and white of the ensigns floating at her tops.

Ever since the two vessels had reached signaling distance, their captains had been supplementing the wireless conversation with International
Code communication. Our excited Italian sailors hoisted string after string
of parti-colored flags in response to the questioning banners flying from
the English halyards, until the captain of the cruiser gave us the word to
proceed.

While the black vessel was drawing away, we suddenly ran into a shower,
whose approach had been unnoticed in the excitement of watching the
cruiser. It blew over in a moment, however; and then, as if to announce
that our war experiences were finally ended, a beautiful rainbow appeared.
After seeing this good omen, we felt that we should have no more "refugee" troubles. Memories of trials on the Continent quickly receded before
thoughts of America, and conversations about the arrival in New York took
precedence over all others during the rest of the voyage.[16]

The next day was filled with repacking bags and suitcases. Suddenly this
idyllic interlude between war and peace was coming to an end for the *Principe
di Udine*'s passengers. On Sunday evening, August 23, after twelve days at sea
under mostly sunny skies, the ship's master, Captain Tiscornia, hosted his
illustrious passengers to a brilliant farewell dinner. In his after-dinner toast, he
said: "Ladies and gentlemen: the friendship which has existed for so many
years between your country and mine makes it most appropriate that you
should be returning home upon an Italian ship. Italy rejoices to be of service
to Americans as America has always rejoiced to serve Italians in their need. If
I have been so fortunate as to have helped you on your way, I am more than
repaid by your friendship, which I assure you, I can never forget. May this voyage of the *Principe di Udine* serve to bind our countries more closely together.
I drink to the health and happiness of the United States and Italy."[17]

The passengers aboard the *Principe di Udine* line the rails and wave their
American flags as their ship arrives in New York City, August 24, 1914.
Photograph from *The Sailing of a Refugee Ship*

On Monday morning, August 24, 1914, murder, rape, pillage, and destruction were banished from the collective thoughts of the *Principe di Udine*'s passengers when they spied the Statue of Liberty welcoming them home. In the
clear brightness of a hot August morning, the *Udine* steamed into New York's
harbor amid geysers of water and blaring whistles from a flotilla of welcoming fireboats. The first chartered steamship of American refugees from Europe
had arrived safely home. Nancy and Ethel crowded the railings along with a
throng of other passengers on the ship's starboard side as tugboats nudged the
Udine into its berth at Pier 59.[18] Hundreds of friends and family waved from
the end of the wharf. The passengers waved their little American flags in
return. A few of the more athletic young men jumped up on the railings, and,
balancing themselves precariously, waved their straw boaters to the crowd
below. A plethora of emotions washed over Nancy: excitement, gratitude, joy,
and a sudden wave of homesickness. Real tears filled her eyes, though she
quickly brushed them away before anyone could see that she was truly crying.

Within an hour of docking, Nancy and Ethel were reunited with their parents, who had come up from Washington the night before. Wasting no more

time than necessary to secure their daughters' mountain of luggage, the over-joyed parents hurried Nancy and Ethel to Penn Station, where they caught the first train south. Annie Johnson was determined that Nancy would sleep in her own bed on her first night home in America.

The following morning, a jubilant Ben Johnson held yet another press conference in his office on Capitol Hill. He had a great story to tell the reporters, even though he did not have all his facts straight.

NANCY JOHNSON REFUSES TO LEAVE BAGGAGE BEHIND. Washington, Aug, 25—Of all the passengers aboard the Principe di Udine, which docked at New York Monday, Miss Nancy Johnson, daughter of Representative Ben Johnson of Bardstown, was the only one who brought all her baggage with her. Men, women and children all over Europe have been abandoning their trunks in their anxiety to be unencumbered, but Miss Johnson served notice to all hands that she traveled when her trunks went and not until.

Miss Johnson reached the home of her parents in Washington, "owing," as her father expressed it, "nearly everyone in the world." Money deposited for her with the State Department never reached Miss Johnson, and she was compelled to borrow money wherever she could. The young woman says that she saw great suffering abroad among Americans, some of them begging in the streets for alms. The condition abroad is considered a disgrace to the Government and, even the Italians, said Miss Johnson, commented upon it and remarked that their Government would take better care of its citizens. Miss Johnson, with Miss Ethel Norris, was in Venice when the war broke out. She traveled into Southern France on her way to Paris and sent a courier ahead to the capital to arrange for transportation. He wired back that he had secured two berths on a ship, which was to sail soon, but Miss Johnson decided that her party had best return to Venice. Fortunately they did this, as the French boat on which her passage was booked never sailed. At Venice the American Consul sent them with an escort to Genoa, whence after three days' waiting they sailed for New York twelve days ago. The boat was small and filled with passengers, all of whom were seasick, but otherwise underwent no hardships. They encountered three submarines, a torpedo boat and two warships, all of which were British. The last warship urged them to run away from any German warship they might encounter, as "there were some in the ocean, out of coal, and they would try to overhaul the Udine and steal their supply."

The Udine was flying the Stars and Stripes all the time.

"We are very proud of Nancy. She showed true Kentucky grit," said Representative Johnson.[19]

There were a number of discrepancies in Johnson's account. Nancy and Ethel never crossed the French border. They turned back to Venice at Lausanne, Switzerland. Their original berths had been booked on the *Re d'Italia*, an Italian liner, not a French one. A photograph in Arno Behnke's firsthand account of the *Principe di Udine*'s crossing shows that Nancy was not the only one who traveled with all her luggage. Nor did Nancy criticize the U.S. government's handling of the crisis overseas. No doubt it was Ben Johnson himself who was exasperated with the government. The American flag was flown only during the second half of the trip, except when the ship was hailed by the British torpedo boat off Gibraltar on August 15. Finally only two British warships stopped the *Udine* on its journey. None of the passengers or crew reported sighting submarines. These were probably Ben Johnson's embellishments. As a canny politician, he was known to occasionally exaggerate the facts in order to make his point.

The following evening Nancy Johnson called the first and only press conference of her life after reading the embellished account of her journey in the morning paper. She and Ethel wanted to set the facts straight. It was the first time that Nancy had ever dared to contradict her father.

DEFENDS THE CONSULS, Warm Praise for U.S. Officials From Miss N. Johnson. Daughter of Kentucky Representative Who Was Caught Abroad by War, Tells How They Turned Consulates Into Lodging Houses and Eating Places, Working Day and Night for Americans.

There is one fair European traveler now in Washington before whom it would be unwise policy to utter a criticism of the conduct of American diplomatic and consular representatives in the war zone in their efforts to afford relief to stranded fellow citizens. She is Miss Nancy Johnson, daughter of Representative and Mrs. Ben Johnson of Kentucky, who was in Venice when war was declared, and who, sailing from Genoa, reached this country a few days ago aboard the Principe di Udine.

With Miss Johnson was Miss Ethel Norris, a Washington girl. In Venice, they were guests of Consul and Mrs. Harvey Carroll, and in Genoa, their interests were looked after by the American consul general, Dr. John Edward Jones, also a Washingtonian.

Nothing Due But Praise. "I am sorry some persons returning to this country have shown a tendency to be critical of the way our representatives abroad managed things in the stressful early days of the homeward rush," said Miss Johnson last night. "There should be no criticism—only praise. I am sure that everything that could be done was done for us and my observation was that everybody who applied to the consulates were [sic] treated just as well as they could have been treated in the circumstances.

"Dr. Carroll, the consul in Venice, opened his own purse to his fellow citizens, and actually impoverished himself in his endeavors to help them. His house was full of people; he allowed them to sleep on the floors, and he turned some of the rooms into regular eating places. He did all kinds of unselfish things, going much further than his government would have requested him to go."

Sacrificed Every Comfort. "It was the same at Genoa, where Dr. Jones had charge as consul general. He remained up for three nights and three days to help Americans, some of them very unreasonable in their demands, and when we said good-bye to him he was almost broken down by loss of sleep.

"Life in Europe when the war began naturally was not 'a bed of roses.' There were hardships to be encountered and any person who expected to have an easy time while the conditions were such as they were could hardly be rated as broadminded."

Miss Johnson said that she would not take a great deal for her experience, now that she is safely back in America.[20]

In actual fact, the experience changed Nancy's life forever.

Epilogue

On Tuesday, September 23, 1914, Nicholas Butler gave a stirring address to the students and faculty at the opening exercises of the 161st session of Columbia University. "Our usual interests however great, our usual problems however pressing, all seem petty and insignificant in view of what has befallen the world," he told the packed hall. "Mankind is back in the primeval forest, with the elemental brute passions finding a truly fiendish expression."

After relating some of his own observations while in France and Switzerland, Butler turned to his main theme. "When exhaustion brings this war to an end, the task of [neutral] America will be to bind up the war's wounds, to soften the war's animosities and to lead the way in the colossal work of reconstruction that must follow. Then, if our heads are clear, our hearts strong, and our aims unselfish . . . we may gain new honor and imperishable fame for our country."[1]

Despite Butler's idealistic sentiments, America eventually joined in the international fray. Overriding his personal desires for neutrality and peace, President Woodrow Wilson, spurred by the continual sinking of American merchantmen without warning, asked Congress to declare war against Germany on April 2, 1917. Some of the first to enlist were nearly all of the 540 men of the Onondaga tribe. Their honor would at last be avenged.

President Wilson's personal life took an upswing. Twenty months after the death of his beloved first wife, Wilson married Edith Bolling Galt on December 18, 1915. Wilson served a second term as president, but he failed to win his country's participation in the League of Nations following the end of the war. He died in 1924.

After experiencing near drowning in January 1914 and fleeing Europe in August, Frederick and Louise Vanderbilt took stock of their lifestyle and decided to retire from New York City's social whirl. They sold their townhouse

THE SAILING OF
A REFUGEE SHIP

A Little record of the voyage of the

PRINCIPE DI UDINE

from Genoa to New York in August,
Nineteen Fourteen, during the first
days of the European Conflict

EDITED BY
ARNO BEHNKE

New York, 1914

Title page of *The Sailing of a Refugee Ship,* privately printed in September 1914

at Fortieth Street and Fifth Avenue in October 1914. The mansion was razed and replaced by a six-story office building housing Arnold Constable & Company. After his experiences in Genoa, Frederick purchased his third yacht, the *Vedette,* within the year following his return to the States. When America entered the war in 1917, Vanderbilt loaned this yacht to the U.S. government. The navy used it as a submarine chaser in the Atlantic. The Vanderbilts helped to equip, clothe, and arm the sixty-five men of the Hyde Park Home Defense. Louise Vanderbilt died while on holiday in Paris in 1926. In 1938, at the age of eighty-two, Frederick followed her in death at their home in Hyde Park. He left an estimated fortune of $54 million.

Arno Behnke published *The Sailing of a Refugee Ship* in September 1914 just before he returned to Dartmouth College to begin his junior year. Behnke's memoir was seventy-eight glossy pages, complete with sixteen black-and-white photographs, several sketches of ships, and a complete passenger list. It was published in a green cloth hardback with the title embossed in gold on the cover. The booklet was paid for by subscription by the passengers.

Behnke graduated from Dartmouth in 1916 with a Bachelor of Science degree. The following year he enlisted in the U.S. Army to fight against the nation that had forced him to flee Europe one summer's day three years earlier. After the war Behnke lived in New York City until 1921, when he became a production assistant, and later a manager, of the Amerada Petroleum Corporation located in Fort Worth, Texas. He married in 1926 and had two daughters. Later in life he enjoyed the pleasure and company of his six grandchildren. He died in Tulsa, Oklahoma, on September 6, 1966. His only publication was his little memoir of his greatest adventure, *The Sailing of a Refugee Ship*.[2]

On October 5, 1914, Nancy received a copy of Behnke's book from a fellow passenger and Washingtonian, Dr. John Boyd. Dr. Boyd inscribed the flyleaf, "For Miss Nancy Johnson, Compliments of the Boyd Family—Oct. 5, 1914." Nancy treasured this gift all her life.

B. Harvey Carroll remained as the American consul in Venice throughout the four years of the war. He gave unstintingly of his time and money to aid his countrymen and women, and, in turn, he received an immortal epitaph from an unexpected source. In May 1918, Carroll chanced to meet a nineteen-year-old American Red Cross ambulance driver who had been wounded while he was passing out chocolate and cigarettes to the Italian soldiers at the Piave River. The driver, Ernest Hemingway, never forgot Carroll's kindness to him. Thirty-two years later, the renowned author mentioned the consul by name in *Across the River and into the Trees,* Hemingway's last full-length novel to be published during his lifetime. "They had a hell of a nice consul here [Venice] in 1918. Everybody liked him. . . . Carroll was the man's name."[3]

The Great War ended on November 11, 1918—at the eleventh hour of the eleventh day of the eleventh month—but it did not end all wars as had been so optimistically hoped. Instead, the seeds of its direct successor were sown before the ink had dried on the Treaty of Versailles. The Second World War began less than twenty-one years later and was even bloodier than the first.

The Iroquois Nation was not invited to the peace talks in Paris, even though they had formally declared war on Germany in 1914. No one took them seriously or thought to include them. Therefore the Iroquois considered themselves still in a state of war with Germany throughout the 1920s and 1930s. When the United States declared war against Hitler's Third Reich in 1941, the Iroquois were ready. Every young man of fighting age enlisted in the U.S. Army and served valiantly during the next four years. In 1945 the Iroquois were finally invited to the peace negotiations in Reims, France. They had been at war with

Germany for more than thirty-two years[4]—the longest state of belligerency of all the nations.

Kaiser Wilhelm II lost his throne, his power, and his empire—though none of his bluster—in the aftermath of the Great War. He was permanently exiled to Holland, where he died in 1941. In an ironic twist of fate, Wilhelm never visited the beautiful city of Paris.

Another leader also suffered defeat and disgrace. In 1915 First Sea Lord Winston Churchill was forced to resign from the British government after the debacle of the ill-conceived campaign at Gallipoli on the Turkish seacoast. Unlike the kaiser, Churchill's political star rose to its zenith in later life when he served as Great Britain's prime minister throughout the darkest days of World War II. When Churchill died in 1965, he was buried with the full honors of a state funeral and mourned not only by the whole British Commonwealth but also by many other nations as well.

One young woman finally realized her own dream of peace at the end of World War I. Her Royal Highness Marie Adelaide, Grand Duchess of Luxembourg, had been appalled by the war's brutish violence. On January 14, 1919, the twenty-five-year-old ruler abdicated in favor of her younger sister, Charlotte. On September 20, 1919, Marie professed her vows as a Carmelite nun and entered the convent in Modena. For the next four years she sought a special closeness with God, until her early death in 1924.

On May 25, 1916, the USS *Tennessee* was renamed the USS *Memphis* so that the name "Tennessee" could be given to a new battleship, hull number 43. Superstitious sailors muttered that it was bad luck to rename a ship. In July 1916, the *Memphis* sailed for Central America on a peacekeeping patrol. It stopped at Santo Domingo, Dominican Republic, in late August. On the afternoon of August 29, as the *Memphis* swung gently at its anchor in the harbor, a freak tidal wave of epic proportions swept up the harbor and smashed the cruiser against the shore. Forty-nine seamen died, and another 204 men were injured. Today the remains of the *Memphis,* formerly the *Tennessee,* are buried under the sandy harbor of Santo Domingo.[5]

On May 29, 1954, forty years after his death, Pope Pius X was canonized a saint in the Roman Catholic Church.

In the summer months of 1914, the world's newspapers carried stories of Kosovo's bid for independence, of gunshots fired in the streets of Sarajevo, and of the presence of soldiers from many nations in the Balkans. In 1998 and 1999, the world's newspapers again carried stories of Kosovo's bid for independence, of more gunshots fired in the streets of Sarajevo, and of the large number of soldiers from many nations once again stationed in the Balkans.

Although Nancy Johnson's personal involvement with World War I was now far behind her, the experience of her harrowing fortnight marked her for the rest of her life. Never again did she take her personal comfort and safety for granted. Her oyster shell of security and privilege had cracked open irreparably. From 1914 on, Nancy's temperament became one of perpetual nervousness, and a new haunted look settled in the depths of her dark eyes. From the time she returned to her parents' apartment on S Street in Washington, D.C., until her death decades later, Nancy, who had enjoyed good health all her youth, was plagued with the migraine headaches that her father and sister Rebecca also experienced, as well as asthma attacks that occurred with depressing regularity over the next fifty years.[6] In the late 1960s, both ailments gradually disappeared.

On November 17, 1915, Nancy married the beau of whom her parents had disapproved, Lieutenant Roscoe Campbell Crawford. President Wilson, preparing for his second marriage a month later, tendered his regrets that he could not attend the wedding of "his personal friend" in Bardstown, but his daughter, Margaret, sent Nancy a large box of flowers from the White House on the morning of Nancy's nuptials.

During the following decades, Nancy and Roscoe had two surviving children and, in time, six grandchildren, six great-grandchildren, and three great-great-grandchildren. Roscoe served in both World War I and II, rising to the rank of major general. Although the Crawford family lived in the Panama Canal Zone and the territory of Hawaii, as well as many other places in the United States, Nancy did not return to Europe for more than twenty years. In 1935 she again sailed across the Atlantic when she accompanied her husband on a six-week tour through Belgium, France, Switzerland, England, and Holland, where Nancy finally visited her Dutch cousins. She also spent several wonderful days in Paris, the goal she had been denied in August 1914. However, she did not return to Italy. During this trip, the Crawfords saw disturbing indications of the preparations for World War II everywhere they went. Nancy was relieved to return to America. She never left it again.

In 1965 Nancy and Roscoe quietly celebrated their Golden Anniversary with their family. Roscoe died in 1980. Nancy followed him in 1982 at the age of ninety-three. They are buried side-by-side in Arlington National Cemetery near their favorite city, Washington, D.C.

Nancy Johnson Crawford outlived all the kings and generals who had changed the map of Europe during the Great War, as well as most of the people who had sailed with her in August 1914 aboard the *Principe di Udine*—the gilded refugee ship.

APPENDIX

"But Think of the Tales They'll Have!"

With elaborate and well-advised measures already taken for the relief and the release of the American tourists who have been caught in the far-flung lines of the European Powers, the anxiety about their whereabouts and safety among friends at home is diminishing and probably soon will cease. There seems to be no doubt that a good many of the wanderers have undergone real hardships, but in no instance, apparently, have their troubles been of the really desperate kind.

Of course it is not pleasant to go without food for a day and a half, to be turned out of hotels with nothing that will be accepted as payment for lodging elsewhere, or to travel many hours in densely crowded trains and extremely mixed company. Help, however, is already in sight for those who have not already received it, and it will not be long before these now much-troubled ones discover that what they have been going through is an adventure rather than calamity—"the experience of a lifetime," as the saying is. Theirs will be the Virgillan [*sic*][1] joys of remembering all these wild happenings, of rehearsing them endlessly to interested relatives and acquaintances at least decently resigned, and of being freed for the rest of their lives from the common necessity of filling in conversational gaps with talk about the weather.

It is no small thing to have been even an involuntary part of historic events, and enviable indeed is he or she who can turn to a page in history and say, "All this I saw and some of it I was!" And for once the unassuming millionaire and the consciously superior schoolma'am [*sic*] have met on the sympathetic level of the strapped and the stumped. Each, presumably, has revealed virtues hitherto unsuspected by the other and they have generously divided their last foolish little francs or marks with reciprocal heroism. We haven't heard much about that yet, but, of course, we soon shall, for only cynics can suspect that it has been a case of "save who can" with the hindmost left to be clutched by the Pursuer.[2]

First Published in the *New York Times*, August 5, 1914

NOTES

Chapter 1: "Bred in Old Kentucky"

1. William Johnson V (1817–1888) was a lawyer and politician, representing Nelson County, Kentucky.

2. Nannie Crow Johnson (1835–1878).

3. See "Highway Marker at Johnson House Unveiled in Ceremony," *Bardstown Kentucky Standard,* November 3, 1981.

4. See Allan M. Trout, "Fabulous Is a Pallid Term for the Late Ben Johnson," *Louisville Courier-Journal,* June 11, 1950.

5. See also Alvin F. Harlow, *"Weep No More My Lady"* (New York: Whittlesey House, McGraw-Hill, 1942), 257, 262.

6. Ben Johnson (1858–1950).

7. Gail MacColl and Carol McD. Wallace, *To Marry an English Lord* (New York: Workman, 1989), 74.

8. "Ben Johnson among County's Most Powerful," in *The Celebration 1792–1992* (Bardstown, Ky.: Bicentennial Publication, 1992), 9.

9. Nelson County, Kentucky, styles itself as the "Bourbon Capital of the World." At one time it was home to over twenty distilleries. In the twenty-first century, the county is still Kentucky's largest producer of bourbon.

10. Johnson family oral history is substantiated by an election souvenir of a little brown whisky jug with "Vote for Johnson" on it. The jug belongs to one of Johnson's descendants.

11. See Harlow, *"Weep No More My Lady,"* 264.

12. Grover Cleveland Bergdoll (1893–1966).

13. See "Ben Johnson 92, Taken by Death," *Louisville Times,* June 5, 1950.

14. Annie Mary Kouwenberg Johnson (1864–1939) came from an old American family on her mother's side. Annie was active in a number of heritage organizations. She was the Kentucky state regent of the Daughters of the American Revolution (DAR), Kentucky state president of the Daughters of 1812, and a member of the Colonial Dames and the Magna Carta Dames.

15. "Mamma's little gun" is now framed in a shadow box that hangs in the home of a descendant.

16. Rebecca Cox Johnson (1887–1961) was born in the family home, Bardstown, Kentucky.

17. Hendy Russell Johnson (1890–1977) was the youngest of the "Johnson beauties." She, too, was born at home in Bardstown. She was named for a family friend.

18. Ben Johnson Jr. (1891–1901) suffered from chronic asthma. Unlike his sisters, he never enjoyed good health.

19. Joseph Cox Kouwenberg (1868–1901) was Annie Johnson's younger brother.

20. In September 1900, at age thirteen, Rebecca had been sent to her mother's alma mater at Loretto Academy, a Catholic girls' boarding school in nearby Marion County.

21. Nannie Crow Johnson [Nancy Johnson] to Rebecca Cox Kouwenbergh, October 29, 1900, Nancy Johnson Crawford Collection (hereafter cited as the NJC Collection; collection in possession of the author).

22. Though Loretto Academy is now gone, the original convent building still stands on a hill in Loretto, Kentucky. In recent times it has been used as a retirement home for nuns. Loretto Village is also the present-day home of the world-famous Maker's Mark Bourbon. The distillery is located next to a stream at the base of the former school's hill.

23. Quotation was attributed to Rebecca by her sister Nancy.

24. In September 1901, Hendy was still attending Bethlehem Academy.

25. Rebecca was starting at Nazareth Academy for her secondary education.

26. Nannie Crow Johnson [Nancy Johnson] to Ben and Annie Johnson, September 5, 1901, NJC Collection.

27. Nancy Johnson's Report Card, Loretto Academy, Loretto, Kentucky, September 30, 1902, NJC Collection.

28. See MacColl and Wallace, *To Marry an English Lord,* 10.

29. Ibid., 137.

30. Unidentified newspaper clipping, NJC Collection. A "barn dance" is close to the modern-day square dance.

31. Advertisements, New National Theatre Program, Washington, D.C., January 13, 1908, and January 25, 1909, NJC Collection. The author recalls dipping into Nancy's omnipresent boxes of candy when she lived with her grandparents. Nancy's love of desserts and sweets was a lifelong passion.

32. "Stricken with Appendicitis," *Louisville Times,* April 14, 1908, NJC Collection.

33. Refers to the annual Continental Congress held every year in Washington, D.C., by the DAR.

34. The pages are usually young women between the ages of eighteen and thirty who act as messengers and personal assistants for the DAR officers during the Congress. Pages traditionally wear white dresses. It is considered a singular honor to be chosen as a page.

35. Constitution Hall, located in Washington, D.C., is the national headquarters for the DAR.

36. "Honor for Miss Johnson," *Louisville Courier-Journal,* April 20, 1908, NJC Collection.

37. Daisy Fitzhugh Ayres was a native of Frankfort, Kentucky, though she lived part of her adult life in Louisville. Prior to her stint as the *Louisville Courier-Journal*'s Washington reporter, she had been a novelist, whose only book, *The Conquest,* was published by the Neale Publishing Company, New York and Washington, D.C., in 1907. It was dedicated to the memory of Daisy's husband, Edward Francis Ayres.

38. Clipping, *Louisville Courier-Journal,* October 21, 1909, NJC Collection.

39. The *Kentuckian* was 430 feet in length and had a 53-foot beam with a 27-foot draft. Its four boilers could speed the ship through the water at twelve knots. The *Kentuckian* was built primarily to carry 8,500 tons of cargo, but it also had cabins for twenty-five passengers. See "Lincoln & Davis Farm Spring Water to Christen Boat," *Baltimore Star,* March 19, 1910, NJC Collection.

40. Helen Herron Taft, wife of the twenty-seventh U.S. president, William Howard Taft (1857–1930).

41. Dante Alighieri (1265–1321), considered to be Italy's greatest poet, wrote the *Divine Comedy* in three parts. The first part, *The Inferno,* describes the seven circles of Hell.

42. See Daisy Fitzhugh Ayres, "Christening Ship Much on the Order of a Wedding," *Louisville Courier-Journal,* March 26, 1910, NJC Collection.

Chapter 2: Going to Europe

1. James Beauchamp "Champ" Clark (1850–1921) was a Democrat from Ohio and the Speaker of the U.S. House of Representatives from 1911 to 1919.

2. "Boys Forever," *Louisville Courier-Journal,* March 2, 1913, NJC Collection.

3. Rebecca Johnson Talbott had little Rebecca (1910) and Naomi (1912), with Ben J. expected in early 1914. Hendy Johnson Hamilton had a single daughter, Hendy Lee, in 1912.

4. See MacColl and Wallace, *To Marry an English Lord,* 136.

5. Wilhelm "William" Frederick Kouwenberg (1839–1930).

6. Maria "Mary" Cornelia Kouwenberg Blaisse (b. 1832).

7. Rebecca Sewell Cox Kouwenberg (1843–1922).

8. Margaret McChord was the daughter of Mr. and Mrs. J. H. McChord of Springfield, Kentucky. J. H. McChord was an active member in the Democratic Party. Margaret would be Nancy's maid of honor in November 1915.

9. B. Harvey Carroll Jr. (1874–1922) served nobly in Venice throughout most of World War I from 1914 to 1918, and later, in Naples, Italy, in 1919.

10. Maria "Mary" Blaisse Martens was the daughter of William's sister, Maria Kouwenbergh Blaisse, making her Nancy's second cousin. Cousin Mary was married to Clemens Martens. Notes from a handwritten Kouwenberg family tree, prepared in Amsterdam, 1935; no birth or death dates given; NJC Collection.

11. Willem Adriaan Blaisse, cousin Mary's older brother. See Kouwenbergh family tree, NJC Collection.

12. Hubert Bartholomeus Blaisse is cousin Mary's younger brother. His wife was Anna Duynstee. They had five children: three boys and two girls. Ibid.

13. Alphonse Jacob Blaisse, Mary's younger brother, and his wife, Stephania "Steph" Omithuysen. Joseph Gerald Blaisse was Mary's youngest brother and was married to his sister-in-law, Dorothea "Dora" Omithuysen. Alphonse and Steph had five children while Joseph and Dora had only four. Ibid.

14. Clemence Martens was Mary's eldest daughter and Nancy's second cousin. This reference to Mary having her "hands full with Clemence" refers to Clemence's preparations to marry Joseph von Hallen-Huber on August 27, 1914. Ibid.

15. "Uncle Adrian" does not appear in the Kouwenbergh family tree, but he may have been a brother to William and Maria, since Maria Blaisse's eldest son was named William Adriaan, perhaps for her two brothers. He might not have been noted in the family tree because he was a celibate priest with no wife or family.

16. William Kouwenbergh to Nancy Johnson, May 23, 1914, NJC Collection.

17. President Woodrow Wilson (1856–1924), the twenty-eighth president of the United States.

18. Pope Pius X (1835–1914) was canonized Saint Pius X in the Catholic Church on May 29, 1954. See Reverend Walter Van de Putte, ed., *Saint Pius X Daily Missal* (New York: Catholic Book, 1956–58), 774.

19. Father William J. Russell to the Right Reverend S. Tampieri, May 25, 1914, NJC Collection.

20. White House invitation to Nancy Johnson, January 13, 1914, NJC Collection.

21. White House wedding announcement to Nancy Johnson, May 7, 1914, NJC Collection.

22. President Woodrow Wilson to Diplomatic and Consular Officers in Europe, May 15, 1914, NJC Collection. This letter was typed on White House stationery but hand signed by the president.

Chapter 3: Innocents Abroad

1. The *Verona* was sunk on November 5, 1918, near Punta di Pellaro. See http://www .roangelo.net/valente/ssverona.html, accessed January 31, 2009.

2. "Kentucky Beauty of Congress Set Sails for Extended Stay in Italy," *Washington Post,* newspaper clipping, May 31, 1914, NJC Collection.

3. *New York Times,* May 26, 1914.

4. At this time, the average worker made $7.00 a week. See Charlotte Ofca Scholl, *Vanderbilt Mansion* (Little Compton, R.I.: Fort Church, 1988), 6.

5. Rebecca Talbott, daughter of Nancy's older sister, Rebecca Johnson Talbott.

6. Nancy Johnson to Ben Johnson, May 26, 1914, NJC Collection.

7. Not true. Nancy did not know Ethel very well before their mothers paired them together for the trip.

8. Daisy Fitzhugh Ayres, "Sails for Venice," *Louisville Courier-Journal,* May 31, 1914, NJC Collection. Also not true. Ben did not know that Mary Martens was not planning to travel from The Hague that summer.

9. Nancy used only one roll of film, thirty-two exposures, on her trip. There were three pictures taken of Nancy and Roscoe Crawford prior to the trip, May 1914; eleven on board the *Verona,* May 27–June 10 1914; seven on the side trip to Monte Carlo, June 14–15, 1914; three on the trip through Milan, June 22–23, 1914; and eight in Venice, July 1914. The roll was developed late July 1914 in Venice. NJC Collection.

10. "Mexican Problem Near Solution," *New York Times,* May 27, 1914.

11. See *New York Times,* May 27, 1914.

12. Ibid.

13. Ibid.

14. Arno Martin Behnke (1892–1966).

15. A copy of this privately published book is in the NJC Collection.

16. Nicholas Murray Butler (1862–1947).

17. Kate La Montague Butler (1865–1948) was Nicholas Butler's second wife.

18. Frederick William Vanderbilt (1856–1938); Louise "Lulu" Anthony Torrance Vanderbilt (1844–1926).

19. "F. W. Vanderbilt Dies in Hyde Park," *New York Times,* June 30, 1938.

20. Information taken from the *Official Guide for the Vanderbilt Mansion, Hyde Park, N.Y.: A National Historic Site* (Washington, D.C.: Government Printing Office, 1999).

21. "F. W. Vanderbilt Dies in Hyde Park."

22. Robert A. C. Smith (1857–1933).

23. See "R. A. C. Smith Dies at 76 in England," *New York Times,* July 28, 1933.

24. See http://books.google.com/books?id=iYdDAAAAIAI&pg=RA1–PAS&dq=marguerite +roby, accessed February 23, 2008.

25. At the top of this letter, Annie Johnson wrote in pencil, "You all read these (if you can) and send to Rebecca. Will send you the post-card later, Mother. Rebecca, please save." This note was probably addressed to Nancy's younger sister, Hendy Johnson Hamilton, to whom Annie had forwarded Nancy's first letter from Italy. Rebecca is Nancy's older sister. The letter was written in black ink on very thin onionskin paper. The ink bled through each side, making the words very difficult to decipher.

26. Foreigners. Nancy mimics one of her father's comic expressions.

27. Spaghetti. Nancy knows her father's horror of "un-American" food.

28. Parmesan cheese. Nancy's children were almost adults before they learned that "powdered cheese" had another name.

29. The presence of icebergs would have been an important subject to Nancy. She was sailing near the spot where the *Titanic* had struck a berg and sank only two years earlier in 1912.

30. Nancy loved being the center of attention.

31. "Dressing" meant wearing formal evening clothes. First-class passengers on the larger liners always dressed for dinner, except for the final evening when their servants needed to pack away their good clothing in the trunks before they were collected on the forward decks for disembarkation. On the more informal *Verona*, the custom of dressing was reversed.

32. Nancy was normally an excellent speller; however, since she never learned how to spell "Gibraltar," she spelled it as she spoke it—with her southern Kentucky accent. The "ar" sound became "a."

33. Nancy probably means the bridge.

34. Morocco; see note on "Gibralta." Later in this letter, Nancy spells Gibraltar correctly.

35. Nancy Johnson to Ben and Annie Johnson, June 5, 1914, NJC Collection.

Chapter 4: The Powder Keg of Europe

1. Kaiser Wilhelm II (1859–1941).

2. Thomas Mann (1875–1955). See S. L. A. Marshall, *The American Heritage History of World War I* (New York: American Heritage, 1964), 9.

3. Barbara W. Tuchman, *The Guns of August* (1966; repr., New York: Bantam Books, 1985), 25–26.

4. Samuel P. Huntington, *The Soldier and the State* (New York: Vintage Books, 1957), 105.

5. See en.wikipedia.org./wiki/Kiel.Canal, accessed January 23, 2009.

6. Alfred von Schlieffen (1833–1913).

7. Tuchman, *Guns of August,* 35.

8. Sir Henry Wilson (1864–1929).

9. Sir Winston Leonard Spencer Churchill (1874–1965).

10. Ferdinand Foch (1851–1929).

11. Steven Jantzen, *Hooray for Peace, Hurrah for War* (New York: Alfred A. Knopf, 1971), 15–16.

12. Colin Simpson, *The Lusitania* (New York: Ballantine Books, 1974), 21.

13. Helmuth von Moltke (1848–1916). He was replaced during the Marne Campaign owing to his ill health, but, more to the point, because he dared to predict that Germany would ultimately lose the war.

14. Arthur T. Vanderbilt II, *Fortune's Children: The Fall of the House of Vanderbilt* (New York: William Morrow, 1989), 223.

15. Charles W. Snell, *Vanderbilt Mansion,* Historical Handbook no. 32 (Washington, D.C.: National Park Service, 1960), 14.

16. Rick Archbold and Dana McCauley, *Last Dinner on the Titanic* (Toronto, Ont.: Hyperion/Madison Press Book, 1997), 25.

Chapter 5: The Fuse Is Lit

1. Henry James, *Henry James in Italy* (New York: Weidenfeld and Nicolson, 1988), 66.

2. John Edward Jones (1869–1918).

3. See Herman W. Know, ed., *Who's Who in New York City and State 1917–1918,* 7th ed. (New York: Who's Who, 1918), 593.

4. Francesco Centorbi, second-class passenger aboard the *Verona.* See *Verona* Passenger List, NJC Collection.

5. Adalgisa Jiana, a second-class passenger aboard the *Verona,* was a schoolteacher bound for Naples. See ibid.

6. Grand Hotel Santa Lucia and Restaurant was still in business in 2009. The building dates from 1907. Modern-day travelers enjoy its romantic charm as well as the views of Naples Bay and Mt. Vesuvius.

7. Approximately $105.10 in 2009.

8. Consul General John Edward Jones.

9. Approximately $52.50 in 2009.

10. Approximately $42,000 in 2009.

11. Prince Luigi Amedeo of Savoy, Duke of Abruzzi (1873–1933), was a handsome Italian prince, as well as a mountain climber and explorer, and a vice admiral in the Italian navy.

12. King Victor Emmanuel III (1869–1947) and Queen Elena (1873–1952; formerly Princess Jelena of Montenegro).

13. The whiskey was in fact Kentucky bourbon, probably distilled in Nelson County where Bardstown is located. Ben Johnson knew the value of bestowing bourbon on his political friends and constituents.

14. Father William J. Russell's letters were the letters of introduction to the Vatican that he wrote for Nancy on May 25, the day she left Washington, D.C., for New York.

15. Clinedinst was the portrait photographer in Washington, D.C., whose photos of Nancy were often used by the newspapers.

16. Julian Potter, son of Mr. and Mrs. Whit Potter of Bowling Green, Kentucky. The Potters were old family friends of Annie Johnson.

17. Nancy slipped in this important bit of information amid a blizzard of inconsequential sentences since she knew her parents would object to this idea.

18. The Berlitz School of Languages began in a one-room schoolhouse in Providence, Rhode Island. The school published phrase booklets to help the traveler learn to speak a foreign language. Daisy Carroll and Nancy had been studying one on the *Verona* in an effort to learn a little Italian.

19. Margaret McChord.

20. Papa is maternal grandfather William Kouwenbergh.

21. Nancy Johnson to Annie Johnson, June 12, 1914, NJC Collection

22. Nancy Crawford, in a conversation with the author, late 1978 or 1979. In 1914 Pope Pius X had been pope for eleven years.

23. Lake Garda, the largest lake in Italy, located halfway between Milan and Venice.

24. James Barclay Young (b. 1884). He married in 1920. His career in the Foreign Service continued through the 1930s.

25. Approximately $84.08 in 2009.

26. Approximately $21,020 in 2009.

27. Prince Albert I of Monaco (1848–1922).

28. Approximately $31.50 in 2009.

29. Nearly seventy years later, Nancy still considered her trip to Venice to be one of the highlights of her life.

30. Mary Blaisse Martens, Nancy's Dutch cousin from The Hague.

31. Daisy Fitzhugh Ayres's flattering article in the *Louisville Courier-Journal* about Nancy's departure on the *Verona.*

32. Nancy Johnson to Ben Johnson, June 23, 1914, NJC Collection.

33. James, *Henry James in Italy,* 57.

34. Hubert Martens, Clemence's brother.

35. "Home" means Annie Johnson.

36. William Grover Sharp (1859–1922), a Democrat from Elyria, Ohio, served in the House of Representatives from 1909 until he resigned in 1914, when he was appointed to serve as the U.S. ambassador to France. The Sharps were close friends of the Johnsons.

37. Leon di Sauvanne.

38. This is a veiled hint that Nancy and Ethel were getting on each other's nerves.

39. Nancy's maternal grandmother, Rebecca Kouwenberg.

40. Ella Kouwenbergh (1871–1965) was Annie Johnson's youngest sister. Ella never married, and she doted on her nieces. She lived with Annie and Ben Johnson for many years, and when Annie died in 1939, Ella remained to nurse Ben Johnson in his old age. "Miss Ella Kouwenbergh, 94, Dies," *(Bardstown) Kentucky Standard,* newspaper clipping, August 19, 1965, NJC Collection. Dan is Dan Talbott, Nancy's brother-in-law.

41. Nancy Johnson to William Kouwenbergh, June 27, 1914, NJC Collection.

42. In 1860, the American consul in Venice noted the same thing: "here discomfort and ruin have their price, and the tumbledown is patched up and sold at rates astounding to innocent strangers who come from countries in good repair and the tumbledown is worth nothing." See John Pemble, *Venice Rediscovered* (Oxford: Clarendon Press, 1995), 22.

43. Nancy's observation is somewhat akin to the pot calling the kettle black.

44. Checks drawn on a bank were not as common as letters of credit in 1914.

45. Ambassador Sharp did not arrive at his post in Paris until September 1914, long after Nancy was forced to return to the United States.

46. Nancy rarely says "please" to her mother, whom she seems to order about in a high-handed manner. On the other hand, she is more coy and sweet to her father, to whom she was much closer.

47. The *Washington Star* was the evening newspaper in Washington, D.C. Apparently Consul General Jones received a bundle of his hometown newspapers from every ship arriving from the United States.

48. Theodore Noyes (1858–1946), publisher of the *Washington Star.*

49. Nancy Johnson to Annie Johnson, June 27, 1914, NJC Collection.

50. See Ayres, "Sails for Venice."

51. Tuchman, *Guns of August,* 91.

52. Prince Otto von Bismarck (1815–1908).

53. "Heir to Austria's Throne Is Slain with His Wife by a Bosnian Youth to Avenge Seizure of His Country," *New York Times,* June 29, 1914.

54. Gavrilo Princip (1894–1918), the son of a postman, suffered from tuberculosis. He died in prison in 1918 while serving his twenty-year sentence.

55. See Marshall, *The American Heritage History of World War I*, 17.

56. Herbert Clark Hoover (1874–1964) was the thirty-first president of the United States.

57. See Edward Robb Ellis, *Echoes of Distant Thunder* (New York: Coward, McCann and Geoghegan, 1975), 144.

58. Ibid., 159.

59. See Heinz Vestner, ed., *Venice, Insight City Guides* (Hong Kong: APA, 1991), 274.

60. Mrs. Ansberry was the wife of Timothy T. Ansberry, Democrat from Defiance, Ohio.

61. Berry & Whitmore Co. were "jewelers, silversmiths, diamond merchants, and art stationers" whose shop was located on the northwest corner of Eleventh and F streets in downtown Washington, D.C. Their motto was "Odd things not found elsewhere," and their store was considered the ideal place to shop for wedding presents. Information taken from an advertisement in the New National Theatre Program (Washington, D.C., February 17, 1908), 10, NJC Collection.

62. Mrs. Beall was the wife of James "Jack" Andrew Beall, a Democrat from Waxahachie, Texas.

63. Josephus Daniels (1862–1948) was Wilson's secretary of the navy from 1913 to 1919.

64. This Margaret was probably Margaret McChord as the Daniels did not have a daughter, only four sons.

65. Ambassador Myron Herrick was at his station in Paris when the war began.

66. Annie Johnson to Nancy Johnson, July 11, 1914, NJC Collection.

67. Maryanne Druin and her sister Margaret were friends of Nancy's from Bardstown, who now lived in Washington, D.C.

68. Approximately $42.04 in 2009.

69. Ben Johnson Talbott (b. March 1, 1914) was Rebecca's third child and first son.

70. Dan Talbott is Rebecca's husband.

71. Nancy Johnson to Rebecca Talbott, July 14, 1914, NJC Collection.

72. Approximately $2,102 in 2009.

73. Approximately $945.90 in 2009.

74. Approximately $420.40 in 2009.

75. Approximately $210.20 in 2009.

76. Nancy Johnson to Ben Johnson, July 16, 1914, NJC Collection.

Chapter 6: The Last Weeks of the Gilded Age

1. Vestner, *Venice*, 256.

2. Arno Behnke, *Sailing of a Refugee Ship* (New York: G. Schirmer, private printing, 1914), 25.

3. See Nancy Johnson to Ben Johnson, July 16, 1914.

4. The author located this bridge in 1993 using the photograph's background as a guide. The buildings behind Nancy in the photo had changed little in nearly eighty years.

5. Number 1300 Ascensione San Marco was home to a bank in 1993. The thirty-two photos, negatives, and the photo shop's envelope are in the NJC Collection.

6. The photo album and the glass vanity jars now belong to the author.

7. Arthur Walworth, *Woodrow Wilson*, 3rd ed., Part 1 (New York: W. W. Norton, 1978), 399–400.

8. Ellis, *Echoes of Distant Thunder*, 158.

9. See John Keegan, *The First World War* (New York: Alfred A. Knopf, 1999), 71.

10. "Noted Refugees on Chartered Ship," *New York Times*, August 25, 1914.

Chapter 7: "A madman wants to change the map"

1. Keegan, *First World War*, 27.
2. "Noted Refugees on Chartered Ship."
3. Behnke, *Sailing of a Refugee Ship*, 41–42.
4. Ibid., 40.
5. Ibid., 41.
6. Marshall, *History of World War I*, 38.
7. Ibid.
8. Ibid.
9. Princess Marie Adelaide, Grand Duchess of Luxembourg (1894–1924).
10. "Drew a Gun on Grand Duchess," *New York Times*, August 10, 1914.
11. Kenneth S. Davis, *FDR: The Beckoning of Destiny 1882–1928* (New York: Random House, 1971), 369–70.

Chapter 8: "It is a king's war"

1. Behnke, *Sailing of a Refugee Ship*, 41–42.
2. "Exhortation to the World to Pray for Peace," *New York Times*, August 20, 1914.
3. See Tuchman, *Guns of August*, 130–31.
4. William E. Volz, "Why Government Should Take Measures to Bring Them Home," *New York Times*, August 4, 1914.
5. The Lloyd Sabaudo Line was formed in Turin, Italy, in 1906 and began its passenger service in 1907. In 1932 the line merged with several other Italian shipping companies to form the Italian Line. See en.wikipedia.org/wiki/Lloyd_Sabaudo, accessed February 7, 2009.
6. SS *Re d'Italia* was built for the Lloyd Sabaudo Line in 1906. It was 430 feet long with a beam of 52.7 feet. It was a 6,560 gross ton ship that had two funnels, two masts, and a top speed of fifteen knots. It carried mainly emigrants from Italy to New York and was scrapped in 1929. See N. R. P. Bonsor, *North Atlantic Seaway*, vol. 3 (Dublin: Brookside, 1975), 1367.
7. Approximately $100 in 1914 dollars, or $2,102 in 2009.
8. See Ellis, *Echoes of Distant Thunder*, 159–60.
9. "Defends the Consuls," *Washington Post*, August 27, 1914, NJC Collection.
10. See Eugene Lyons, *Herbert Hoover: A Biography* (1948; repr., New York: Doubleday, 1964), 75.
11. "Noted Refugees on Chartered Ship."
12. Approximately $2,102 in 2009.
13. Laugieri to Nancy Johnson, telegram, August 3, 1914, NJC Collection.
14. See Nancy Johnson to Ben Johnson, July 16, 1914.
15. See Ellis, *Echoes of Distant Thunder*, 159.
16. Ibid., 159–60.
17. Behnke, *Sailing of a Refugee Ship*, 42.
18. "President Advises Nation to Be Calm," *New York Times*, August 4, 1914.
19. Marshall, *History of World War I*, 58.
20. See Hanson W. Baldwin, *World War I: An Outline History* (New York: Harper and Row, 1962), 18.
21. Meirion Harris and Susie Harris, *The Last Days of Innocence: America at War 1917–1918* (New York: Random House, 1997), 137.

Chapter 9: "I want a ship that's westward bound"

1. Chapter title taken from the poem "America for Me," by Henry van Dyke.

2. See Jill D. Duvall, *The Onondaga* (Chicago: Children's Press, 1991).

3. Harris and Harris, *Last Days of Innocence*, 137.

4. See Ellis, *Echoes of Distant Thunder*, 159.

5. Canada, one of Great Britain's dominions, entered World War I on August 4, 1914, when Great Britain declared war on Germany. Canada did not declare war independently.

6. Ellis, *Echoes of Distant Thunder*, 155–56.

7. Tuchman, *Guns of August*, 152.

8. Ibid., 147.

9. Ibid., 153.

10. Laugieri asked for $340.00, or $7,146.80 in 2009.

11. Laugieri to Nancy Johnson, telegram, August 4, 1912, NJC Collection.

12. Behnke, *Sailing of a Refugee Ship*, 2.

13. Laugieri to Nancy Johnson, telegram, August 5, 1914, NJC Collection.

14. See "Noted Refugees on Chartered Ship."

15. Ibid.

16. Ben Johnson sent $500 to Nancy, according to her during a conversation with the author in the late 1970s. The sum is equal to $10,510 in 2009.

17. "Kentuckians in Europe Are Safe," *Louisville Times*, August 6, 1914, NJC Collection.

18. Johnson's $500 in gold disappeared entirely, according to Nancy Crawford.

19. "R. A. C. Smith Dies at 76."

20. Gano Dunn (1870–1953). See "Gano Dunn Is Dead; Noted Engineer, 82," *New York Times*, April 11, 1953.

21. James, *Henry James in Italy*, 65.

22. Approximately $60,000 in 1914; approximately $1,261,200 in 2009.

23. Approximately $100,000 in 1914; approximately $2,102,000 in 2009.

24. Ellis, *Echoes of Distant Thunder*, 161.

25. Approximately $210,200 in 2009.

26. Approximately $1,891,800 in 2009.

27. Approximately, in 2009 figures, $250 would be $5,255, $100 would be $2,102, and $50 would be $1,051. See Behnke, *Sailing of a Refugee Ship*, 9–10.

28. August 11, 1914, the day before the *Principe di Udine* was due to sail.

29. Edward Jones to Nancy Crawford, telegram, August 5, 1914, NJC Collection.

30. "Gold Cruiser to Sail Today," *New York Times*, August 6, 1914.

31. Approximately $168,160,000 in 2009.

32. Henry S. Breckinridge (1884–1960). In 1914 Herbert Hoover, who helped with the American refugee relief program in London, called Breckinridge "a more complete idiot than whom I have yet to discover in public office." See George H. Nash, *Life of Herbert Hoover: The Humanitarian* (New York: W. W. Norton, 1983), 11.

33. "Gold Cruiser to Sail Today."

Chapter 10: Gilded Refugees

1. See Walworth, *Woodrow Wilson*, 400.

2. Edward Jones to Nancy Johnson, telegram, August 7, 1914, NJC Collection.

3. Edward Jones to Ben Johnson, hand-written telegraph message from State Department, August 10, 1914, NJC Collection.

4. See "She Will Quit Genoa," *Washington Post,* newspaper clipping, August 12, 1914, NJC Collection.

5. Approximately $1,261,200 in 2009.

6. See Behnke, *Sailing of a Refugee Ship,* 66.

7. Nancy Crawford, in a conversation with the author in the early 1980s.

8. These men included: Horace E. Andrews, president of the New York State Railway and a director of the New York Central Railway, making Andrews a personal friend of Vanderbilt, who owned the New York Central Railway. Dr. Edwin Beer, urological surgeon at Mt. Sinai Hospital, New York. Dr. John C. Boyd of Washington, D.C., retired medical director, U.S. Navy. Gustave Schirmer of New York, book publisher who subsequently published Arno Behnke's memoir, *The Sailing of a Refugee Ship.* Stephen Lane Folger of New York, one of the founders of the Standard Oil Company (now Exxon Corp.), brother of Henry Clay Folger, founder of the Folger Shakespeare Library in Washington, D.C., and a cousin to the Folger Coffee family. Park Benjamin of New York (1849–1922), an official of the U.S. Patent Office. He graduated from the U.S. Naval Academy at Annapolis, Maryland, in 1867. He designed the Naval Academy's official seal and the motto that was adopted in 1899. He was also the future father-in-law of the renowned tenor Enrico Caruso, whom Benjamin loathed. See Park Benjamin obituary, *New York Times,* August 22, 1922. George B. "Max" McClellan Jr., son of the famous Union general George B. McClellan. Max was the mayor of New York City from 1903 to 1909. In 1914 he was a professor at Princeton University in New Jersey. When he was mayor, he arranged for the creation of the world-famous Times Square. See George McClellan obituary, *New York Times,* December 1, 1940. Theodore W. Noyes, publisher of the *Washington (D.C.) Star.*

9. See "Bought a Ship for Trip Home," *Louisville Times,* August 25, 1914, NJC Collection.

10. Approximately $315,300 in 2009.

11. Approximately $378.36 for a ton of coal in 2009.

12. See "Charter a Ship to Bring Americans," *New York Times,* August 19, 1914.

13. See "Cabled Money Held Up," *New York Times,* August 9, 1914.

14. Behnke, *Sailing of a Refugee Ship,* 6–7.

15. "Tourists Flock into Genoa," *New York Times,* August 19, 1914.

16. "But Think of the Tales They'll Have!" *New York Times,* August 5, 1914.

17. See "5,000 Stranded in Italy," *New York Times,* August 18, 1914.

18. Nancy Crawford, in conversations with the author in the late 1970s.

19. Behnke, *Sailing of a Refugee Ship,* 49.

20. See "Had a Thrilling Time but Came Through in Safety," *Louisville Evening Post,* August 26, 1914, NJC Collection.

21. Behnke, *Sailing of a Refugee Ship,* 52.

22. "She Will Quit Genoa."

23. Behnke, *Sailing of a Refugee Ship,* 54.

24. Ibid., 26.

25. Ibid., 22.

26. Ibid., 33.

27. Ibid., 34–35.

28. See "Edwin Thanhouser Dies," *New York Times,* March 23, 1956.

29. Behnke, *Sailing of a Refugee Ship,* 43.

Chapter 11: America for Me

1. See Behnke, *Sailing of a Refugee Ship*, 17–45.
2. Approximately $2,102,000 in 2009.
3. "Had a Thrilling Time but Came Through in Safety."
4. Behnke, *Sailing of a Refugee Ship*, 61–62. In October 1914, Nancy highlighted these paragraphs in her copy of Behnke's book.
5. See *New York Times*, August 16, 1914. Information obtained from www.gjenvick.com/Ö/1914Sailing-RefugeePassengerList.html, accessed October 2, 2009.
6. See "Get $415,000 Gold to London Refugees," *New York Times*, August 18, 1914.
7. Ibid.
8. "The Pope Ill in Bed," *New York Times*, August 17, 1917.
9. Behnke, *Sailing of a Refugee Ship*, 57.
10. Ibid., 58.
11. "Pope Pius X Dies at 1:20 This Morning," *New York Times*, August 20, 1914.
12. Behnke, *Sailing of a Refugee Ship*, 61.
13. Nancy Crawford in a conversation with the author in the early 1980s.
14. Behnke, *Sailing of a Refugee Ship*, 63–64.
15. HMS *Caronia* information, see "http://en.wikipedia.org/wili/RMS_Caronia_(1905), accessed October 2, 2009.
16. Behnke, *Sailing of a Refugee Ship*, 64–65. Nancy underlined these passages in her copy of Behnke's book. In a conversation with the author, she said that this was probably the most exciting moment of the entire voyage for her.
17. Ibid., 66.
18. See ibid., photograph, 67.
19. "Nancy Johnson Refuses to Leave Baggage Behind," *Louisville Courier-Journal*, August 26, 1914, NJC Collection.
20. See "Defends the Consuls."

Epilogue

1. See "World's Hope Lies in U.S., Says Butler," *New York Times*, September 24, 1914.
2. Obituary, *Dartmouth Alumni Magazine*, November 1966. See also obituary, *Tulsa (Okla.) World*, September 5, 1966.
3. Ernest Hemingway, *Across the River and into the Trees* (1950; repr., New York: Collier Books, 1978), 73.
4. See Angie Debo, *A History of the Indians of the United States* (Norman: University of Oklahoma Press, 1970).
5. See Edward L. Beach Jr., *The Wreck of the Memphis* (1966; repr., Annapolis, Md.: Naval Institute Press, 1998).
6. Several elder members of Nancy's family concurred with the onset of Nancy's headaches and asthma as well as her general nervousness.

Appendix

1. The Roman poet Virgil (70–19 B.C.E.) wrote *The Aeneid*, a long epic poem that told of the wanderings and adventures of Aeneas (Ulysses) for twenty years after the fall of Troy until he finally reached his wife and home.
2. This appendix was originally published as "But Think of the Tales They'll Have!"

BIBLIOGRAPHY

Books

Archbold, Rick, and Dana McCauley. *Last Dinner on the Titanic.* Toronto, Ont.: Hyperion / Madison Press Books, 1997.

Baldwin, Hanson W. *World War I: An Outline History.* New York: Harper and Row, 1962.

Balsan, Consuelo Vanderbilt. *The Glitter and the Gold.* 1953. Reprint, Maidstone, Kent, England: George Mann, 1973.

Barraclough, Geoffrey, ed. *The Times Concise Atlas of World History.* London: Times Books, 1982.

Beach, Edward L., Jr. *The Wreck of the Memphis.* 1966. Reprint, Annapolis, Md.: Naval Institute Press, 1998.

Behnke, Arno. *Sailing of a Refugee Ship.* New York: G. Schirmer, private printing, 1914.

"Ben Johnson among County's Most Powerful." In *The Celebration 1792–1992.* Bardstown, Ky.: Bicentennial Publication, 1992, 9.

Bonsor, N. R. P., ed. *North Atlantic Seaway.* Vol. 3. Dublin: Brookside, 1975.

Burner, David. *Herbert Hoover: A Public Life.* New York: Alfred A. Knopf, 1978.

Churchill, Winston S. *The World Crisis.* New York: Charles Scribner and Sons, 1923.

Clare, John D., ed. *First World War.* New York: Gulliver Books, Harcourt Brace, 1995.

David, Daniel. *The 1914 Campaign: August-October 1914.* New York: Military Press, 1987.

Davis, Kenneth S. *FDR: The Beckoning of Destiny 1882–1928.* New York: Random House, 1971.

Debo, Angie. *A History of the Indians of the United States.* Norman: University of Oklahoma Press, 1970.

Duvall, Jill D. *The Onondaga.* Chicago: Children's Press, 1991.

Eggenberger, David. *An Encyclopedia of Battles.* 1967. Reprint, New York: Dover, 1985.

Ellis, Edward Robb. *Echoes of Distant Thunder.* New York: Coward, McCann and Geoghegon, 1975.

Graymont, Barbara. *The Iroquois.* New York: Chelsea House, 1988.

Gregory, Alexis. *The Golden Age of Travel: 1880–1930.* New York: Rizzoli, 1990.

Harris, Meirion, and Susie Harris. *The Last Days of Innocence: America at War 1917–1918.* New York: Random House, 1997.

Hemingway, Ernest. *Across the River and into the Trees.* 1950. Reprint, New York: Collier Books, 1978.

Huntington, Samuel P. *The Soldier and the State.* New York: Vintage Books, 1957.

James, Henry. *Henry James in Italy.* New York: Weidenfeld and Nicolson, 1988.

Jantzen, Steven. *Hooray for Peace, Hurrah for War.* New York, Alfred A. Knopf, 1971. Reprint, New York: Facts on File, 1991.

Keegan, John. *The First World War.* New York: Alfred A. Knopf, 1999.

Know, Herman W., ed. *Who's Who in New York City and State 1917–1918.* 7th ed. New York: Who's Who, 1918.

Lyons, Eugene. *Herbert Hoover: A Biography.* 1948. Reprint, New York: Doubleday, 1964.

MacColl, Gail, and Carol McD. Wallace. *To Marry an English Lord.* New York: Workman, 1989.

Mann, Thomas. *Death in Venice.* New York: Vintage Books, 1936.

Marshall, S. L. A. *The American Heritage History of World War I.* New York: American Heritage, 1964.

"Mexican Problem Near Solution." *New York Times,* May 27, 1914.

Nash, George H. *Life of Herbert Hoover: The Humanitarian.* New York: W. W. Norton, 1983.

Pemble, John. *Venice Rediscovered.* Oxford: Clarendon Press, 1995.

Ross, Stewart. *Origins of World War I.* New York: Bookwright Press, 1989.

Scholl, Charlotte Ofca. *Vanderbilt Mansion.* Little Compton, R.I.: Fort Church, 1988.

Sears, Stephen W. *George B. McClellen: The Young Napoleon.* New York: Tinker and Fields, 1988.

Simpson, Colin. *The Lusitania.* New York: Ballantine Books, 1974.

Snell, Charles W. *Vanderbilt Mansion.* Historical Handbook no. 32. Washington, D.C.: National Park Service, 1960.

Stokesbury, James L. *A Short History of World War I.* New York: William Morris, 1981.

Tomphison, Vincent, ed. *American Decades 1910–1919.* Detroit: Gale Research, 1996.

Trout, Allan M. "Fabulous Is a Pallid Term for the Late Ben Johnson." *Louisville Courier-Journal,* June 11, 1950.

Tuchman, Barbara W. *Guns of August.* 1962. Reprint, New York: Bantam Books, 1988.

Vanderbilt, Arthur T., II. *Fortune's Children: The Fall of the House of Vanderbilt.* New York: William Morrow, 1989.

Van de Putte, Reverend Walter, ed. *Saint Pius X Daily Missal.* New York: Catholic Books, 1958.

Vestner, Heinz, ed. *Venice, Insight City Guides.* Hong Kong: APA, 1991.

Walworth, Arthur. *Woodrow Wilson.* 3rd ed. New York: W. W. Norton, 1978.

Winter, Jay, and Blaine Baggett. *The Great War and the Shaping of the 20th Century.* New York: Penguin Studio, 1996.

Articles and Newspapers

"Arno Martin Behnke, 1916." Obituary, Class Notes, *Dartmouth College Alumni Magazine,* November 1966.

Ayres, Daisy Fitzhugh. "Christening Ship Much on the Order of a Wedding." *Louisville Courier-Journal,* March 26, 1910.

———. "Sails for Venice." *Louisville Courier-Journal,* May 31, 1914.

"Ben Johnson, 92, Taken in Death." *Louisville Times,* June 5, 1950.

"Bought a Ship for the Trip Home." *Louisville Times,* August 25, 1914.

"Boys Forever." *Louisville Courier-Journal,* March 2, 1913.

"But Think of the Tales They'll Have!" *New York Times,* August 5, 1914.

"Cabled Money Held Up." *New York Times,* August 9, 1914.

"Charter a Ship to Bring Americans." *New York Times,* August 19, 1914.

"Citizens of Capital Sailing from Italy." *Washington Star,* August 12, 1914.

"Consuls to Obtain Ships for Refugees." *Washington Times,* August 12, 1914.

"Defends the Consuls." *Washington Post,* August 27, 1914.

"Drew a Gun on Grand Duchess." *New York Times,* August 10, 1914.

"Edwin Thanhouser Dies." *New York Times,* March 23, 1956.

"England May Put on Stricter Censorship." *New York Times,* August 7, 1914.

"Exhortation to the World to Pray for Peace." *New York Times,* August 20, 1914.

"F. W. Vanderbilt Dies in Hyde Park." *New York Times,* June 30, 1938.

"5,000 Stranded in Italy." *New York Times,* August 18, 1914.

"Gano Dunn Is Dead." *New York Times,* April 11, 1953.

"Get $415,000 Gold to London Refugees." *New York Times,* August 18, 1914.

"Gold Cruiser to Sail Today." *New York Times,* August 6, 1914.

"Had a Thrilling Trip but Came Through in Safety." *Louisville Evening Post,* August 26, 1914.

"Heir to Austria's Throne Is Slain with His Wife by a Bosnian Youth to Avenge Seizure of His Country." *New York Times,* June 29, 1914.

"Highway Marker at Johnson House Unveiled in Ceremony." *Bardstown Kentucky Standard,* November 3, 1981.

"Honor for Miss Johnson." *Louisville Courier-Journal,* April 20, 1908.

"Kentuckians in Europe Are Safe." *Louisville Times,* August 6, 1914.

"Kentucky Beauty of Congress Set Sails for Extended Stay in Italy." *Washington Post,* May 31, 1914.

"Lincoln and Davis Farm Spring Water to Christen Boat." *Baltimore Star,* March 19, 1910.

"London Honoring American Drafts." *New York Times,* August 6, 1914.

"Miss Ella Kouwenberg, 94, Dies." *Bardstown Kentucky Standard,* August 19, 1965.

"Miss Nancy Johnson Is Soon to Sail for U.S." *Louisville Courier-Journal,* August 11, 1914.

"Miss Nancy Johnson Soon to Sail for U.S." *Bardstown Kentucky Standard,* August 13, 1914.

"Mrs. Wilson Dies in White House." *New York Times,* August 7, 1914.

"Nancy Johnson Refuses to Leave Baggage Behind." *Louisville Courier-Journal,* August 26, 1914.

"Noted Refugees on Chartered Ship." *New York Times,* August 25, 1914.

"Pope Pius X Dies at 1:20 This Morning." *New York Times,* August 20, 1914.

"President Advises Nation to Be Calm." *New York Times,* August 4, 1914.

"President's Wife Gravely Ill." *New York Times,* August 6, 1914.

"R. A. C. Smith Dies at 76 in England." *New York Times,* July 28, 1933.

"Returns from Italy." *Washington Star,* August 25, 1914.

"She Will Quit Genoa." *Washington Post,* August 12, 1914.

"Ships Leaving Italian Ports." *New York Times,* August 16, 1914.

"Stricken with Appendicitis." *Louisville Times,* April 14, 1908.

"The Pope Ill in Bed." *New York Times,* August 17, 1914.

"Took Official as Spy." *Washington Post,* August 10, 1914.

"Tourists Flock into Genoa." *New York Times,* August 19, 1914.

"Tourists Held in Italy." *New York Times,* August 10, 1914.

Trout, Allan M. "Fabulous Is a Pallid Term for the Late Ben Johnson." *Louisville Courier-Journal,* June 11, 1950.

Volz, William E. "Why Government Should Take Measures to Bring Them Home." *New York Times,* August 4, 1914.

"Week of Gayety [*sic*] for Younger Set in Washington." *New York World,* April 3, 1910.

"Wilson Asks Absolute Neutrality." *New York Times,* August 19, 1914.

"World's Hope Lies in U.S., Says Butler." *New York Times,* September 24, 1914.

INDEX

ABOUT THE AUTHOR

A native of Washington, D.C., MARY W. SCHALLER is the award-winning author or editor of sixteen books and plays, including *Soldiering for Glory: The Civil War Letters of Colonel Frank Schaller, Twenty-second Mississippi Infantry.* Schaller's books have collectively sold more than one million copies worldwide and several have been translated into other languages. She lives in Burke, Virginia, with her husband, Martin.